The 30 Day Whole Foods Slow Cooker Challenge

Delicious, Simple, and Quick Whole Food Slow Cooker Recipes for Everyone

D1455282

Table of Contents

Welcome to the 30 Day Whole Foods Slow Cooker Challenge!

Thank you for choosing to buy this book, and congratulations in joining the thousands of people who have improved their health and increased their energy and enthusiasm by changing their outlook on food and eating habits.

I used to think I ate a fairly healthy diet. I would shop organic, search for the best brands and shortest lists of ingredients for prepared foods, and eat only at the more upscale fast-food establishments. But I still suffered from poor digestion, bloating, and the feeling of always craving just a little something more. I was lethargic, and always seemed to go down with whatever illness was making the rounds.

I knew I must be doing something wrong. But what?

The truth is that I thought I was paying attention and keeping to a healthy diet, but I wasn't. Like everyone these days, I am always in a hurry. Before I started the Whole Foods Slow Cooker Challenge, I'd dash in from work, open the freezer and throw a pre-packaged meal in there. Or worse, I'd pick up something to go and eat it in the car!

One day I was complaining to a friend about my bloating, bad digestion, and tiredness and she asked if I had heard of the Whole Food diet. I had, and had even considered taking the challenge, but when I saw all those recipes with their long lists of ingredients and instructions I knew I was out of my depth. I loved the idea of eating healthier, but I'm not an expert in the kitchen. Plus, who has the time to cook every meal from scratch? Not me!

If only there was a simple Whole Foods diet; a diet that allowed me to cook with the same ingredients - whole foods - but with recipes that didn't require much cooking skill, and even less time in preparation ...
Enter the 30 Day Whole Foods Slow Cooker Challenge! An easier, more practical twist on the original diet, this challenge has the same benefits but with recipes that are healthy and simple to prepare. In this diet, the ingredients are simply tossed in the slow cooker and left alone to cook. When you're ready to eat - Voila! A healthy, satisfying meal is ready and waiting.

I eagerly accepted this new, easier challenge and a month later I was feeling more energetic, and had lost my snack cravings almost completely. Even better, I'd lost weight without trying! And my bloating and poor digestion were gone. I started searching for more recipes so I could continue the diet, and eventually had collected enough that I decided to share my favorites and create my own Whole Foods Slow Cooker cookbook for you.

Are you ready to take the 30 Day Whole Foods Slow Cooker Challenge?

Let's go!

Explaining the 30 Day Whole Food Slow Cooker Challenge

Simply put, the 30 Day Whole Foods Slow Cooker Challenge is a simple, easy way to eat right, lose weight, and gain more energy and enthusiasm for life.

Based on the Whole Food 30 Day Challenge created by sports nutritionist David Hartwig and his wife Melissa, the 30-Day Whole Foods Slow Cooker Challenge takes the whole food diet requirements and re-imagines them in recipes designed for a slow cooker.

Each recipe can be prepared in 30 minutes or less, then slow cooked while you take care of the other priorities in your life. This book has a selection of slow cooker recipes for breakfast, lunch and dinner to cover the entire 30 days of your diet. Recipes are divided into sections for breakfast, entrees, soups, sides, and some special holiday dishes. You'll find meat, poultry, fish and vegetarian options as well as some sneaky snacks to help you when you really need some comfort food.

Break poor eating habits and addictions.

You may have tried diets before and failed. Or maybe you succeeded, but once the diet was over you immediately fell back into your old habits. What these diets fail to acknowledge is that food is much more than a physical need. We all know that eating can make us feel happier when we're sad, or comfort us during times of stress. We associate certain foods with great times in our lives or people we love. Food is more than nourishment, and eating can be a psychological addiction that is hard to break.

The 30-day Whole Foods Slow Cooker Challenge acknowledges that changing your diet means breaking eating patterns that have been built up over decades. Your commitment to this diet is a commitment to cutting out the foods that are destroying your body. Bloating, indigestion, low energy and general overall malaise are symptoms of poor diet that can be fixed by targeting the food groups that cause these symptoms. You will learn to read your body, and understand that the cravings you feel are not necessarily in your best interest! Minimizing the sugars, grains, dairy and legumes on your plate will break your bad diet habit, introducing you to a new way of eating your favorite foods.

Make your commitment!

Your life can change with this diet, but you have to commit to the challenge. The results may be amazing, but nothing will happen without your desire to make it so. You will not change without wanting to change!

Do you want this? Are you serious about committing to this diet? If you are, this book is designed to help you.

A 30-day challenge means just that: for four weeks you must eat only the recipes in this book. You may struggle as your sugar addicted body sends you false messages and tempts you to fulfill your toxic cravings by sneaking unhealthy snacks. Don't do it!

I know that breaking habits is hard, so this book makes keeping to the Whole Foods diet as easy as possible. It has been designed to help you overcome your challenges with:

- An easy check list of what to eat and what not to eat.
- Whole foods basics grocery list to stock your pantry with the most important ingredients for your new diet.
- 58 easy to prepare slow cooker recipes that make eating healthily fast and simple.
- A holiday meal menu, with all the traditional favorites!
- A snack section with sneakily healthy recipes that will satisfy your cravings.

Get ready to hit the reset button on your habits and re-train yourself into a new, healthier way of eating. Follow the easy, healthy and delicious recipes in this book for just four weeks, and you'll discover a more vital, energized, healthy (and thinner!) you!

The Benefits of Whole Food Slow Cooking

Detox Yourself - Detox Your Lifestyle

You may have heard of conscious eating, and this is an essential element of the Whole Foods challenge: eating not only whole foods, but in a holistic manner. It is one of the one diets that connects mind, body and spirit so that you not only to eat healthier for your physical well-being, but embrace a healthier lifestyle that brings you more contentment and calm in every part of your life.

In 30 days you will eliminate the contaminates that have built up in your body from decades of eating processed and hard to digest foods. Selecting only whole foods for your diet allows your body to heal, and regain the levels of energy and vitality that are a healthy and natural way of being. Your stress levels will decrease, and you will find yourself able to stay calmer and less easily irritated when small things go wrong in your day. The whole food diet has been proven to help with the symptoms of dozens of diseases, and pin-point the cause of many food-related allergies.

When your body is no-longer fighting against the irritants and toxins that are in so many modern foods it is able to devote more energy to parts of the body that have been neglected. Think of your body as a garden that was once filled with flowers and beautiful plants, but has been neglected and overgrown by weeds. It is a constant struggle for the original plants to find light and nutrients to grow, and they are hidden in the tangle of invasive weeds. Remove the weeds and the plants no longer have to fight! They have the space and light to grow tall and once more flower and fill the garden with beauty. So tear out the weeds of toxic foods and embrace a healthy, wholesome and holistic diet!

A Short History of Slow Cooking

Once upon a time, slow cooking was the main way to prepare a meal. For the countless ages before we had custom-built kitchens with ovens and cook-tops, dinner was prepared in a giant iron cauldron over burning fire. This pot would be tended constantly, and hungry workers could eat from it as soon as they walked in from the fields. Oats, vegetables, and small game such as rabbits were common ingredients and the resulting stew would change flavors based on what was available. This tradition is honored in the nursery rhyme "Pease porridge hot, pease porridge cold, pease porridge in the pot, nine days old!"

While pease porridge might not sound so appetizing, having hot, nourishing food available when you want it does. Modern cooking picked up the roots of slow cooking in 1936 when inventor Irving Naxon was inspired by his grandmother's tales of cooking Cholent, a traditional Jewish dish that is simmered overnight so that it could be eaten on the Sabbath without requiring preparation. I have included the recipe for a traditional Cholent in this book, so you can try this delicious, rich, slow cooked stew!

To make Cholent and other traditionally slow cooked foods such as bean crock, Naxon created a cooking device that was portable and provided an even heat to cook foods at low temperatures. This device, called 'Naxon's Beanery' was patented in 1940. Although popular, it was the feminist revolution of the 1970's that made the slow-cooker a must have kitchen appliance. The slow-cooker solved the challenge of working full-time and making home-cooked meals, and simplified home-cooking for career-focused singles.

In the 1990's and early 2000's the slow-cooker was eclipsed by newer, shinier kitchen appliances and its use was mostly limited to spicy pot-luck dips and chili. Today, the whole foods revolution has taken the crock-pot out of the party circuit and made it the center-piece of a new way of eating: The 30 Day Whole Foods Slow Cooker Challenge!

The Benefits of Slow Cooking

I have already talked about how cooking with a slow cooker makes the sometimes complicated and time-consuming recipes of the whole foods challenge more straight-forward and faster to create, and how this makes the whole challenge itself more accessible to everyone. However, slow cooking has benefits above and beyond those of easing and simplifying the challenge of switching to a whole foods diet. Compared to traditional methods, slow cooking is...

Cheap!

Many slow cooker recipes use cheaper cuts of meat, as they are tenderized by the long stewing process. In fact, slow-cooking tougher meats often makes them taste better than more expensive cuts cooked using a traditional method.

Efficient!

Slow cookers are much more energy efficient that traditional cooking. A slow cooker draws uses approximately 0.7 kw of power over 8 hours of cooking, which is only slightly more than one electric bulb would use over the same time span. The difference is that leaving your porch light on while you're at work won't make you dinner, but leaving your slow cooker bubbling will! Some slow-cookers add to their efficiency with built-in timers, allowing you to set a time for the cooker to start, stop, or raise and lower the cooking temperature while you are gone.

Clean!

Single pot cooking means less dishes, which is both a time-saver for you, and a help for the environment. Also, the lower temperatures of a slow cooker mean you avoid the burned, cooked hard glazes and crusts that make traditional pans need soaking and scrubbing. No-one will argue that having fewer, easier to clean dishes makes everyone happy!

Easy!

If you find cooking lengthy, elaborate dishes a challenge, then like me, you will love that the simplicity of slow cooker recipes means you have almost zero chance to mess-up! If you can handle basic ingredient preparation, you are qualified to make any slow cooker recipe. There are no sauces that could lump or curdle, no sensitive sautéing, burned pans, or pots boiling over. In fact, slow cooking makes it almost impossible to ruin your dinner!

The Whole Food Slow Cooker Challenge Rules

What are Whole Foods?

Whole foods are the opposite of processed foods; foods that are as close to their natural state as possible. A hundred years ago, before the coming of preservatives, flavorings and color, our diets were almost completely whole foods. Today however, finding foods in their natural state can be tough. So get ready to read labels! Even the most innocent seeming products, whose brands state natural, organic, or healthy on the label can actually be full of sugar, processed grains, and other non-whole foods.

A general guideline is that you can eat unlimited vegetables, unprocessed meat, fish, shellfish, eggs, olive and coconut oil, and ghee. You can also eat fruit, nuts (except peanuts), and seeds in moderation.

Drink options include water (switch to unflavored sparkling water if you find it hard to quit your soda habit) black coffee and tea, coconut juice, fruit and vegetable juice in moderation.

As a major part of the whole food diet is cutting out sugar entirely, you want to limit your intake of sweeter items such as dried fruit. Sugars are often 'hidden' in packaged foods. If in doubt check the percentage of sugars listed on nutritional label. Any sugar is too much!

In a dream world, avoiding pre-packaged foods entirely is the ideal. But eating only items that are natural or made from scratch is sometimes impractical or impossible. For example, canned or packaged is pretty much the only way to get coconut unless you have a coco palm in your yard and are willing to climb it with a machete in your teeth!

So get into the habit of always checking the ingredients list when buying packed products. Common additives and preservatives you need to stay clear of are sugars (of course), sulfites, carrageenan, and the well-known flavor enhancer mono-sodium glutamate (MSG). If you don't recognize all the ingredients on the label as whole food compliant, don't eat it.

While some pre-packaged products can be made entirely with 'good' whole food ingredients, bear in mind the whole food analogy of SWYPO (Google it!) which cautions against trying to replicate junk foods with whole food ingredients. The point of this diet is not to make the items you are used to eating whole food compliant, but to change the way you eat and break your poor eating habits. In other words, controlling your desire is more important than if you keep your pants on or not!

A Quick Whole Foods Yes/No Guide

Here are some easy to remember examples of whole foods vs common non-whole foods. You can print out this list to post it in your kitchen somewhere where you can easily refer to it. An active forum on what is and is not whole food friendly is available on the Whole30 website in the "Can I Have ..." section.

Remember the golden rules: No sugar! No unknown ingredients!

Whole Foods

- Natural cuts of meat, preferably organic, grass-fed or naturally raised
- Naturally smoked or salt-cured meats
- Natural seafood, preferably from a sustainable source
- Eggs, preferable free-range
- Vegetables
- Fruit and unsweetened fruit juice
- Nuts and seeds
  (in limited amounts)
- Fresh pod legumes. These are legumes eaten with their pod, such as snap peas and green beans
- Dried and fresh herbs, spices, and salt
- Black coffee and teas
- Vinegar
- Coconut in any form: butter, oil, milk, meat, dried or canned.
- Animal fats, clarified butter or ghee, olive oil, avocado oil
- Some approved pre-packaged whole food compliant meals, in moderation

Non Whole Foods

- Processed meats with added sugars, sulfites, MSG, or carrageenan
- Surimi (fake crab) sticks, processed fish and fish products with added sugars, sulfites, MSG, or carrageenan
- All dairy products, including milk, cheese, butter etc. Also non-dairy creamers
- Junk food, including 'healthy' junk food
- All sugars and sugar substitutes including honey, stevia, agave syrup, coconut sugar, etc.
- All grains, including gluten free grains
- Legumes, including all beans, peas, chickpeas, lentils, and peanuts
- Spice mixes with sugars or sulfites, MSG, carrageenan
- Sodas and sugar-added juices, alcohol in any form
- Pickled items
- Soy products, including soy milk, soy sauce
- Vegetable oil, peanut oil, mixed oils

Grocery List Essentials

The first real step in your 30 Day Whole Foods Slow Cooler Challenge is to go through your fridge and larder and throw out or hide away those tempting sugar-filled snacks and junk foods. You know the stuff I'm talking about! Not having these things easily available will help you avoid temptations or mistakes when you are preparing your meals. This diet is strict. If you mess up, you start over... so it's best to be prepared and start off with a kitchen filled with only whole food compliant foods. Which means that...

Step two is to go grocery shopping! As you are just starting out learning what foods are whole food compliant or not, we have created a list of the basic items to buy. You will need to supplement these with the specific ingredients for each week's meals, but this will make sure you have the staples in stock. Following the guidelines from the Whole30 website, I have divided my list into four sections: Proteins, Vegetables, Fruits, and Fat. You will probably have most of the required spices and herbs already in your pantry – just check for added sugars and MSG before using any spice mixes or rubs.

Proteins

Protein is an important part of the 30 Day Whole Food Slow Cooker Challenge. This list specifies organic, sustainably raised meats but if you don't have a store near you that has these meats then you can substitute the highest quality, leanest meats you can find. Of course, if you can do it, the ideal is meat or fish you have caught yourself!

- 100% Grass-fed, Organic meats: beef, buffalo, lamb, elk, venison etc.
- Pasture-raised, Organic Meats: Pork, rabbit, wild-boar etc.
- Pasture-raised, Organic Poultry: Chicken, turkey, duck, quail etc.
- Pasture-raised, Organic Eggs
- Pasture-raised/Grass-fed, Organic, Natural Processed Meats: Bacon, ham, sausage, pepperoni, etc.
- Sustainable Seafood: Shrimp, tilapia, salmon, clams etc. Check http://www.seafoodwatch.org for sustainable and wild-caught seafood options.

Vegetables

All vegetables are whole foods, so feel free to indulge in all your favorites! You are going to want to introduce new veggies, so the list below includes some whole food diet staples that you may not have tried before. My favorite innovation from doing this challenge was learning to love zucchini noodles, known as zoodles. I used to be a pasta fan, but no longer!

15

As well as discovering new ways to use familiar vegetables, test out these lesser-used occupants of your grocery store produce section:

- Acorn squash
- Anise root (Fennel)
- Avocado
- Buttercup squash
- Butternut squash
- Jicama
- Olives
- Pumpkin
- Spaghetti squash
- Summer squash
- Sweet potato (Yam)
- Swiss chard
- Watercress

Fruits

Although, like vegetables, all fruits are whole foods, you should limit the amount in your diet to two servings per day. Rather than eating fruits alone as a 'dessert' include them in other recipes as a natural sweetener or to add flavor. You may be used to adding sugar to your spaghetti sauce, but half a diced apple will cut the acid without the need for processed sweetness.

Staple fresh fruits to keep in stock are:

- Apples
- Bananas
- Berries: Raspberries, Blueberries, Strawberries etc.
- Dates
- Figs
- Citrus: Lemon, Lime, Orange, Grapefruit
- Pears
- Pomegranate
- Watermelon

Note: All-natural dried fruit and fruit pastes may be used in moderation.

Fats

- Animal Fats: Suet (Tallow), Lard, Duck fat, Schmaltz (chicken fat)
- Milk derived fats: Clarified butter, Ghee
- Vegetable fats: Coconut oil, Coconut butter, Macadamia nut butter, Sunflower seed butter, Extra-virgin Olive oil

Note: Avocados and olives are officially considered 'eating fats' but I have included them under vegetables in my list as they are more commonly considered produce.

Nuts and Seeds

Considered 'eating fats' all nuts and seeds are whole foods, but some can be eaten more freely than others.

- Eat freely: Cashews, Coconut meat (fresh and dried) and milk, Hazelnuts (Filberts), Macadamias
- Eat in moderation: Almonds, Brazil nuts, Pecans, Pistachios
- Eat Sparingly: Flax seeds, Pine Nuts, Pumpkin Seeds (Pepitas), Sesame Seeds, Sunflower Seeds, Walnuts

Get Ready to Start Your Challenge!

There are a few additional things you need to know before you get cooking. First and most importantly, let's clarify...

The Rules

1. Eat ONLY Real Food
It's not about nutritional facts, calories or fat content any more. It's all about the ingredients. You must know every single ingredient that is in every bite of food you are eating. No mysteries, no hidden additives or sneaked in sugars. KNOW WHAT IS IN YOUR FOOD. Period.

2. Organic, Sustainable Food is Best.
Shopping responsibly is not just about helping the earth and protecting the environment: It's about helping yourself and protecting your health. While they may be whole foods, produce and meats raised though intensive methods in huge industrialized farms are more likely to have hidden hormones, include traces of pesticides, or be genetically modified.

3. Fat is Not the Enemy.
In the last few decades we have demonized fat and idolized sugar, replacing the richness and flavor given by natural fats with partially hydrogenated horrors, fake flavors, and the ever present corn syrup. In the whole foods diet you will once again embrace whole fats such as lard, suet, clarified butter, ghee, nut butters, and nut oils. Foods high in healthy fats, such as avocados, cashews, macadamias, coconut meat, and olives are allowed in unlimited quantities. You are welcome!

4. No Sugar Means NO Sugar.
Not honey, not sugar substitutes. No maple syrup, agave nectar, coconut sugar, stevia, Splenda, equal, NutraSweet, xylitol ... If it's a sweetener, then it's not allowed. The closest you can get is date puree, but that's to be used in moderation. If you can't live without chocolate, see if you can find whole roasted cacao beans to give you that endorphin rush. They're bitter, but they are chocolate!

5. No Alcohol, and No Tobacco.
Quitting your food addictions is no good if you're going to continue with other unhealthy habits in your life so any alcohol and tobacco products are completely off the menu. This can double or triple the intensity of an already tough diet, so we recommend that heavy

smokers or habitual drinkers take it step by step and quit their primary addictions before attempting the 30 Day Whole Food Slow Cooker Challenge. That said, only you know how firm your resolve can be, and a few strong-willed people have successfully quit the triple threat of tobacco, alcohol, and sugar all at once.

6. Cheat, and Start Over.

A bit like the board game chutes and ladders, if you make one misstep you slide back to square one and start again. This means that if you cave and eat a chocolate chip cookie on day 29 ... the next morning you're counting from day one again. All participants in the challenge are expected to commit fully to the diet – no cheating, no exceptions. Of course, the only person you cheat if you eat forbidden items is yourself, but then you are the most important person of all.

The Plan

I personally don't like diets where you are given exact menus with recipes for every meal, every day of the week. I like to be flexible with what I eat, and choose each meal based on my activities for that day. So rather than following the arbitrary menus decided by an anonymous author I create my own weekly menu by choosing dishes from the recipes in this book. Below is an example of a weekly meal plan I put together. In the appendix you'll find a blank sheet that you can complete yourself.

Day \ Meal	Monday	Tuesday	Wednesday	Thursday	Friday	Saturday	Sunday
Breakfast	Meaty Breakfast Loaf	Shakshuka Eggs	Date and Nut N'Oatmeal	Mini Quiche Peppers	Stuffed Sweeties	Cockadoodle Zoodle Soup	Perfect Brunch Frittata
Lunch	A slice of cold breakfast loaf and salad.	Cold Thai Chicken Wings and spiralized cucumber with salt and lime dressing.	Zoodles Primavera with the last of the meaty breakfast loaf on the side.	Left-over Yes! Lasagna with salad.	Left-over Mini Quiche Peppers with salad	Left over Pescado Braziliano with a side of Cauliflower Risotto	Beef Pot Roast
Snack	Spicy Snack Almonds			Steamy Plantains			Sweet Fruit Sauce
Dinner	Thai Chicken Wings	Texas Taco Soup	Yes! Lasagna	Moroccan bacon soup	Pescado Braziliano	Slow-cooked Shrimp 'Fettuccini'	Tacos Carnitas

Note: Most cooking times in this book have been given for the low heat setting on your slow cooker. If you need to cook a dish faster, a general rule of thumb is to half the cooking time for high heat. But be careful! If you're cooking at a higher heat you may need to add more liquids to avoid your dish becoming dry.

The Goal

Every success seminar that has ever been teaches that you can't reach a goal unless you know what it is. What are your goals? Write down three reasons you are taking this challenge. Three things you want to change in your life. Do it right now!

I am taking this challenge because:

1. _____
2. _____
3. _____

Breakfast Recipes

Good morning! You are probably going to find the biggest change in your diet happens here, in the first meal of the day. This diet places a lot of emphasis on eating a good breakfast, and no grains or dairy means that most fast breakfast stand-by are not allowed.

But who said breakfast had to be cereal or toast? Not me! I actually love eating the previous night's left-overs for breakfast. Quickly heated on the stovetop, or if I am in a rush, cold straight from the fridge. Soup is another non-traditional get-up-and-go meal, and I have shared a delicious recipe for Cockadoodle Zoodle soup with you.

But don't worry if these unconventional choices don't appeal to you, there are no restrictions on eating eggs during 30 Day Whole Foods Slow Cooker Challenge and in this chapter you'll find many innovative ways to cook them in a slow cooker. I've also included some recipes for grain-free oatmeal (known as n'oatmeal) for those days when you just need some warm, comforting nourishment to start your day. N'oatmeal tends to be higher in sugar than other breakfast foods, so don't eat it every morning.

Egg and Meat Breakfasts

Meaty Breakfast Loaf

A hearty breakfast for meat lovers, this recipe gives you a whole food compliant breakfast slice. Just don't add jam! This recipe uses ground turkey, but you can easily make this dish with ground pork - just change meats and switch out the tomato with 1 tsp dried red pepper flakes.

Prep time: 10 mins
Cook time: 3 hours
Serves: 4
Ingredients:

- 2 lb. ground turkey meat, preferably pasture-raised and organic
- 2 large eggs, preferably pasture-raised and organic
- 1 small tomato, diced, or a tbsp. of tomato puree
- 1 tbsp. each of fresh sage, oregano, and marjoram*
- 1 tbsp. ground paprika
- Coconut oil for frying
- 1 yellow onion, finely chopped
- 3 medium-sized garlic cloves, finely diced
- ¼ cup finely minced pecans

If you do not have fresh herbs, 1 tsp of dried herb can be substituted

Method:

1. Put the ground turkey meat, eggs, tomato, herbs and spices in a medium mixing bowl.
2. In a medium sized skillet, heat the coconut oil and sauté the diced onion until it is clear. Add the garlic and pecans, and sauté for another 3-4 minutes.
3. Add the garlic onion mixture to the mixing bowl, and with clean dry hands blend the mixture together so that all ingredients are evenly distributed.
4. Press the blended mixture together to form a rough ball shape.
5. Do not over mix, too much handling will make the meat tough.
6. Transfer the meat mixture into your slow cooker, and mold it into a rectangular loaf shape. You can actually make the loaf any shape you prefer, just be sure it is not touching the sides of the cooker.
7. Cook on low for 3 hours, then remove the loaf and place on a cutting board to cool.
8. When it is cool enough to handle, cut it into slices and enjoy!
9. Do not allow the loaf to sit too long in the cooker after it is done, as this will dry it out.

Left-overs can be stored in the fridge and re-heated by browning in a skillet with a tsp of coconut oil.

Cockadoodle Zoodle Breakfast Soup

Soup for breakfast! Weird, right? But challenges are about trying new things, so don't knock it until you've tried it. I eat this warm and nourishing soup when I need a morning pick-me-up, maybe when I'm a little under the weather or whenever I need instant comfort and energy.

This recipe makes a lot of soup, so if you are cooking for one or two and don't want left-overs, use chicken pieces rather than a whole bird. Just make sure you have bones to give the stock flavor and add nutrients.

It's guaranteed to cure what ails you!

Prep time: 10 mins
Cook time: 10 hours
Serves: Lots!

Ingredients:
- 1 large onion, diced
- 1 large carrot, diced
- 1 fresh, pasture-raised, organic chicken (approx. 4 lbs.)
- 1 tsp tarragon
- 1 tsp sage
- 1 tsp cumin
- Salt and pepper, to taste
- 5 - 6 pints cold water (use bone broth if you want a richer soup)

Toppings:
- 1 cup fresh cilantro or parsley, finely chopped
- 1 cup red onion, finely diced
- ½ avocado, chopped
- 1 fresh lime, quartered

Method:
1. Peel and dice the onion and carrot.
2. Place the chicken, vegetables and seasonings in your slow cooker and slowly pour in the water or broth. Do not skimp on the liquid.
3. Cook on a low heat for 8-10 hours, or overnight.

4. You can tell the chicken is done when the meat is falling off the bones.
5. Okay, here you have two choices. You can scoop yourself a bowl of the broth, add toppings to taste and enjoy!

Or ...

6. Carefully remove the chicken carcass from the pot and set aside in a large bowl to cool.
7. Make sure you have removed all the bones and gristle from the broth by scooping it with a slotted spoon.
8. Debone the cooled chicken carcass, pulling the meat off with a fork and shredding it.
9. Put the chicken meat back into the broth, and save the bones to make stock later.
10. Serve the soup with a sprinkle of diced onion, cilantro, avocado and a squeeze of fresh lime.

Note: This dish needs a 6 quart slow cooker to be able to fit enough water to simmer the chicken overnight. If your slow cooker is smaller, then adjust the amount of chicken accordingly.

Sakshuka Eggs

Shake up your morning with this traditional middle-eastern breakfast that spices up poached eggs deliciously. You can add or subtract ingredients to the base sauce to make this dish your own. I like to stir in some fresh spinach just before adding the eggs for an extra vitamin boost.

Prep time: 15 mins
Cook time: 3 hours + 15 minutes
Serves: 2-4

Ingredients:

- ¼ cup extra-virgin olive oil,
- ½ an onion, sliced thinly
- 3 cups tomatoes, diced
- 3 garlic cloves, sliced thinly
- ½ tsp paprika
- ½ tsp cayenne pepper
- ¾ tsp cumin
- Bay leaf
- Salt and pepper, to taste
- 4-6 large eggs, preferably pasture-raised and organic
- Parsley, chopped (for garnish)

Optional:

- 1 jalapeño pepper, seeded and minced
- 2 cups roasted peppers, sliced thinly
- 2 cups fresh spinach
- 1 cup carrots, diced

Method:

1. Coat the bottom of the slow cooker with the olive oil, and add the vegetables, herbs and spices. Stir to combine.
2. Cook on high for 3 hours, or until the ingredients have cooked into a nice soft sauce.
3. Crack the eggs directly into the sauce, cover and cook for another 10 - 15 minutes, or until the egg whites are opaque and set but the yolks are still bright yellow and soft.

4. Depending on the number of people you are feeding (or how hungry you are), you can add as many or as few eggs as you like. Just make sure each egg has enough sauce surrounding it that it can cook without touching its neighbors or the sides of the cooker.

5. Carefully scoop out each cooked egg separately, and serve in a low bowl with parsley sprinkled on top.

Porky Breakfast Pie

This is a delicious egg dish that hits all the breakfast highs. Customize it by adding your favorite vegetables. I like bell peppers to add color, or a seeded, diced jalapeno for some spice. If you have any sauce left over from your Shakshuka eggs, heat it up and serve it over this pie for a rich addition.

Prep Time: 10 mins
Cook Time: 8 hours
Serves: 4-6

Ingredients:
- 1 onion, diced
- 1 medium zucchini, diced
- 1 sweet potato (yam), grated
- coconut oil
- 1 lb. natural, organic, breakfast sausage (pork, turkey, or venison)
- 2 cloves garlic, finely diced
- 1 tbsp. fresh basil, chopped
- Salt and pepper, to taste
- 8 eggs

Method:
1. Prepare the vegetables. I sometimes 'cheat' by coarsely chopping them then 'whizzing' them together in my food processor. Just make sure the sweet potato is finely chopped or grated so you don't get chunks.
2. Coat the base and sides of the crockpot with coconut oil to help prevent the pie from sticking.
3. Tip the vegetables, meat, spices, and herbs into the crockpot.
4. Beat the eggs, and add them to the crockpot. Stir everything together.
5. Cook on low for 6-8 hours, or until the eggs are cooked and fluffy and the meat is completely cooked.
6. Carefully remove the inside pan from the slow cooker, tip the pie onto a plate and serve!

Perfect Brunch Frittata

I don't know about you, but I love the combination of spinach and mushrooms. It used to be my go-to pizza topping, but since that's a no-no on the 30 Day Whole Foods Slow Cooker Challenge I make this brunch frittata instead. It's definitely way better than cold pizza in the morning!

Of course, as with all the recipes in this book, you can swap the veggies out however you want. Just don't use tomatoes, bell-peppers, or other 'watery' veg in this recipe, as too much moisture as the eggs cook will ruin the texture. Serve with some fresh fruit, cantaloupe and strawberries give that authentic brunch experience, or for a tropical twist try a fresh pineapple, mango, or papaya.

Prep time: 15 mins
Cook time: 2 hours
Serves: 2-4

Ingredients:
- 4 mushrooms, sliced
- 1 cup fresh spinach
- 2 garlic cloves, finely diced
- Coconut oil
- 6-8 eggs
- Salt and pepper, to taste

Method:
1. Prep the vegetables.
2. Coat the inside of your slow cooker with a small amount of coconut oil.
3. Beat the eggs, and tip into the slow cooker.
4. Add other ingredients and stir to combine.
5. Cover and cook on high for 2 hours or until the eggs are set.
6. Carefully remove the inside pan from the slow cooker, tip the frittata onto a plate and serve!

Mini Quiche Peppers

I've always loved stuffed peppers, and so this take on the traditional dinner dish caught my eye. Here the peppers take the place of pastry and are filled as if they were mini quiches. I think this is a perfect dish for a fun family brunch, and these peppers travel well for an unusual cold picnic snack. Vegetarians can swap the ham for mushrooms or other vegetables.

Prep time: 15 mins
Cook time: 3 hours
Serves: 2-4

Ingredients:
- 2 large bell peppers, halved and seeded
- 1 cup fresh spinach, chopped
- ½ cup onion, finely diced
- 1 cup naturally cured ham, diced
- 6 eggs
- Salt and pepper, to taste
- 1 tsp paprika

Method:
1. Prepare vegetables and ham.
2. Whisk eggs with salt, pepper and paprika in a medium bowl.
3. Add ham, spinach and onion to the eggs and combine.
4. Line inside of slow cooker with parchment paper and place the pepper halves on it.
5. Carefully fill each pepper with the egg mixture.
6. Cover and cook on low for 3 hours, or until the peppers are soft and the eggs are set.

No-Egg Breakfasts

N'Oatmeal

No-oat oatmeal, known as n'oatmeal, has become a popular recipe for people searching for non-grain alternatives for breakfast. There are many variations out there, but I like this one best because it doesn't rely on 'pseudo grains' such as flaxseed and chia to give it a thick oatmeal-like texture. Although n'oatmeal has plenty of flavor as is, feel free to add your favorite toppings.

Prep Time: 10 minutes
Cook Time: 8 hours
Servings: 2-4 servings

Ingredients:
- ½ cup raw walnuts, soaked and blended
- ½ cup raw almonds, soaked and blended
- 1 medium butternut squash, peeled and cubed
- 2 medium apples, peeled and cubed
- 1 cup dates, chopped
- 1 tsp cinnamon
- ¼ tsp nutmeg
- 1 cup coconut milk

Suggested Toppings:
- Dried fruit
- Powdered cinnamon
- Natural powered cacao
- Desiccated coconut
- Toasted pecans
- Fresh berries
- Sliced fresh fruit

Method:

1. Soak the nuts in filtered, salted water overnight.
2. Drain and rinse the nuts, then blend until they have a mealy consistency.
3. Peel and chop the butternut squash and apples, and chop the dates.
4. Put all the ingredients in your slow cooker, cover and cook on low for 8 hours (or overnight).
5. Serve in a bowl with toppings as you desire. :-)

Note: If your n'oatmeal isn't as smooth as you'd like you can mash it with a potato masher, or use a hand blender to get a really creamy texture. I mix mine by retaining half unblended and mixing it back it in after blending the other half.

Stuffed Sweeties

One of the most popular breakfasts on the 30 Day Whole Foods Slow Cooker Challenge is also the simplest: Baked and stuffed sweet potatoes.

Prep Time: 10 minutes (including toppings)
Cook Time: 8 hours
Servings: Varies

Ingredients:
- As many sweet potatoes as you can comfortably fit in your slow cooker

Optional Toppings:
(These toppings are suggestions, feel free to stuff your sweetie however you choose!)
- Fresh blueberries
- Pomegranate seeds
- Chia seeds
- Fresh mango, peeled and diced
- Fresh kiwi, peeled and diced
- Dried blueberries
- Dried cranberries
- Hazelnuts, chopped
- Almonds, chopped
- Apple, diced
- Cinnamon

Method:
1. Clean the sweet potatoes by scrubbing them in fresh water. Do not peel them or dry them.
2. Lay the damp potatoes on the base of your slow cooker, making sure they fit comfortably in one layer without overlapping.
3. Cover and cook on low for 8 hours, or overnight.
4. Carefully remove each potato individually, and cut lengthways.
5. Fill with toppings as you choose, or see the suggestions below.

Traditional Sweeties
6. Core and dice two crisp green apples and toss the cubes in cinnamon until completely coated. Divide evenly between the potatoes.

Tropical Sweeties

7. For an even sweeter sweetie top with diced ripe mango and pineapple chunks.

Nutty Sweeties

8. Sprinkle 1/4 cup dried blueberries or cranberries and 1/4 cup coarsely chopped almonds and/or hazelnuts over the potatoes.

Superfood Sweeties

9. Sprinkle a cup of blueberries and ½ a cup of pomegranate seeds evenly between the potatoes, then add a small amount of chia seeds to add a little texture.

Breakfast Pudding

Sweet potatoes, dried coconut, and apples are the secret in this thick, warming breakfast that hits the spot when you've just about had it with eggs. There's no sugar in this dish, although the natural sweetness of the ingredients might have you convinced otherwise.

Prep Time: 10 mins
Cook Time: 4 hours
Servings: 4-6 servings

Ingredients:

- 2 large eggs, preferably pasture-raised and organic
- 1 tsp cinnamon
- ¼ tsp nutmeg
- Pinch salt
- ¼ inch fresh ginger, peeled and grated (or 1 tsp ginger powder)
- ½ cup coconut milk
- 1 large sweet potato, peeled and grated
- 1 large or 2 medium crisp apple(s), cored, peeled and grated
- ½ cup dried coconut
- ¼ cup raisins, halved
- Coconut oil
- ¼ cup toasted pecans, chopped

Method:

1. Beat the eggs, and add the spices, ginger, and coconut milk. Whisk until well combined.
2. Stir in the grated sweet potato, apple, dried coconut, and raisins.
3. Grease the inside of your slow cooker with coconut oil.
4. Pour the egg mixture into the slow cooker, cover, and cook on low for about 4 hours or until the eggs have set and the ingredients have combined to a smooth consistency.
5. Serve warm, with a sprinkling of chopped pecans.

CocoLoco Pears

This 3-step breakfast is about as easy as it gets. Just throw the ingredients in the slow cooker and wake up to the delicious aroma of baked pears with a tropical twist.

Prep Time: 5 minutes
Cook Time: 8 hours
Servings: 4-6

Ingredients:
- 6 ripe pears, deseeded and chopped
- 3 cups coconut, shredded
- 1 ½ cups coconut milk
- 1 cup fresh pineapple, chopped (optional)
- ⅔ cup coconut butter
- 2 tbsp. coconut oil
- 1/2 tsp cinnamon
- ¼ tsp nutmeg
- Pinch of salt

Method:
1. Put all ingredients into your slow cooker, and stir together.
2. Cook on low for 8 hours, or overnight.
3. Wake and eat!

Banana Nut Custard

This creamy breakfast dish is a satisfying start to the day, and a delicious treat when you are craving a spoonful of something sweet. Just don't eat it all at once!

Prep Time: 15 minutes
Cook Time: 4 hours
Servings: 4-6

Ingredients:
- 2 cups sweet potatoes, grated
- 2 cups coconut milk
- 2 very ripe bananas
- 4 eggs
- 3 tbsp. nut butter (almond is my favorite)
- Pinch of salt
- Cinnamon to taste
- Coconut oil
- Fresh nutmeg, grated (optional)

Method:
1. Grate the sweet potatoes, and place into a large mixing bowl or blender with the coconut milk, peeled bananas, eggs, nut butter, salt and cinnamon.
2. Blend together until you have an even consistency (The sweet potato may not mix in completely, but everything else should by blended with no clumps).
3. Grease the inside of your slow cooker lightly with a coating of coconut oil.
4. Pour the mixture into the slow cooker, cover and bake for 4 hours, or until the eggs are set and the pudding has a gelatinous consistency.
5. Pour into a serving dish and allow to cool.
6. Serve warm or cold, with a sprinkle of grated nutmeg on top.

Soups and Sides

Eating whole foods doesn't mean eating heavily. The slow cooker was designed for soups and stews, and there are many delicious and healthy recipes that are perfect for a light lunch or evening meal. I have included some of my favorites here for you. I hope you like them!

Soups

Texas Taco Soup

Want your taco fix without the corn shell or soft flour burrito? This spicy southern soup manages to taste like a taco, but it's loaded with whole foods and vitamins instead of mystery meat and additives!

Prep Time: 15 minutes
Cook Time: 8 hours
Servings: 6-8

Ingredients:
- 1 ½ tbsp. ghee (or other fat)
- 1 onion, peeled and diced
- ½ cup diced jalapenos (add more if you like your tacos spicy!)
- 3 ½ cups fresh Roma tomatoes, diced
- ½ cup green bell pepper, diced
- ½ cup orange bell pepper, diced
- ½ cup red bell pepper, diced
- 1 cup carrots, diced
- 2 cloves of fresh garlic, minced
- 2 tbsp. cumin
- 2 tsp sea salt
- 2 tsp black pepper
- 1 tsp paprika
- 1 tsp red pepper flakes
- 1 tsp cinnamon
- ½ tsp garlic powder
- ½ tsp oregano
- ½ tsp onion powder
- ¼ tsp cayenne
- 3 cups bone broth
- ¾ cup coconut milk

Options for meat:
- 2 lbs. chicken breast, preferably pasture-raised and organic * **OR**
- 2 lbs. minced lean beef, preferably pasture-raised and organic *

* This recipe can be made with beef or chicken, or for a lighter soup just omit the meat altogether.

Optional Toppings:
- Avocado, chopped
- Fresh cilantro, chopped
- Red onion, diced
- Whole coriander seeds, dried
- Pickled jalapeno 'rajas'
- Fresh limes, sliced
- Homemade 'Pico de Gallo' salsa (diced tomatoes, cilantro, and onions marinated with a squeeze of lime)

Method:
1. If you are cooking with beef, then sauté the onions and jalapenos in the melted ghee until the onions start to go clear, then add the beef and stir until browned. Drain the excess water from the meat with a fine mesh colander.
2. If using chicken, sauté the breasts with the onions and jalapenos until just cooked through.
3. Place all the ingredients, including the cooked beef or chicken, into the slow cooker and stir together.
4. Cover and cook on low for 7-8 hours or overnight.
5. Stir before serving. If using chicken, it should separate into strands, if it doesn't then either cook longer or carefully shred with a fork.
6. Serve with toppings as desired and a slice of fresh lime juice floating on top. Provecho!

Winter Salmon Soup

Not all slow cooker meals are slow. This warm and creamy salmon soup is a simple and fast lunch or an elegant first course for a dinner menu. Pair with a crisp green salad.

Prep Time: 10 mins
Cook Time: 4 hours + 15 mins
Servings: 4- 6

Ingredients:
- 1 lb. salmon fillets, sustainably fished, cut into 1 inch chunks
- 3 leeks, cleaned and sliced into think rounds
- 2 carrots, julienned
- 3 cloves garlic, minced
- 6 cups fish stock (chicken stock can be used in a pinch, but fish is best)
- 2 tsp dried thyme leaves
- 1 bay leaf
- 1¾ cup coconut milk
- Salt & pepper, to taste

Method:
1. Add all ingredients except the salmon into the slow cooker.
2. Cover and cook on low for 4 hours.
3. Add the salmon and re-cover. Cook for a further 15 minutes or until the salmon is opaque pink.
4. Serve immediately.

Louisiana Cajun Gumbo

Send your taste buds down to the bayous of southern Louisiana with this whole food twist on traditional Cajun gumbo. Although I hope you love the spice mixture in this recipe, you might want to play with the different rations of spices and herbs to find the perfect taste for you. Just remember that the spice level will increase as the gumbo simmers in the slow cooker. Laissez les bon temps rouler!

Prep Time: 10 minutes
Cook Time: 6-8 hours plus 15 minutes
Servings: 6-8

Ingredients:

- 1 lb. shrimp, peeled (save shells and heads)
- 2 lbs. boneless skinless chicken thighs, chopped into ½ inch cubes.
- natural smoked sausage, cut into half-moon rounds
- 1 cup green bell pepper, diced
- ½ cup red bell pepper, diced
- 1 sweet Vidalia onion, diced
- 2 celery stalks, diced (optional)
- ½ cup fresh okra, diced (optional)
- 4 garlic cloves, minced
- ½ tsp dried red pepper
- ½ tsp black pepper
- ½ tsp cayenne
- ½ tsp garlic powder
- ½ tsp sweet paprika
- ¼ tsp dried oregano
- ¼ tsp ground cumin
- ¼ tsp onion powder
- 4-5 pints fresh water
- Salt and pepper, to taste
- Tabasco sauce, to taste
- Gumbo filé (optional)

Method:

1. Peel and shell the shrimp and put them in the fridge, keeping the shells (and heads if you have them) out.
2. Prepare all other ingredients as in the list above, including mixing the spices together. *
3. Put the vegetables, chicken, sausage, and spices in the slow cooker.
4. Add water, making sure the meat and veg mixture is covered plus some.
5. Add the bag or strainer with the shrimp shells and submerge it in the liquid.
6. Cover and cook low for 6–8 hours, or overnight.
7. Carefully remove the shrimp shells, and taste the broth. Add salt, pepper and Tabasco to taste.
8. Add the shrimp and gently stir. Cover and cook for an additional 15 minutes or until the shrimp are cooked.
9. Serve in wide bowls with a sprinkle of gumbo filé on top. Bon appetit!

If you want to increase the quantities and make your own Cajun spice mix, add salt to the spices as you mix them. I make my spice mix in the ratio 12:1. So for every 12 oz. of salt, I add 1 oz. each of black pepper, red pepper, cayenne, garlic, and sweet paprika and ½ oz. oregano, cumin, and onion powder. This makes it spicier and less salty, so you can adjust the ratio according to your taste.

Moroccan Bacon Soup

This is an unusual soup with a flavor that melds sweet and spice. The sweet potato makes it creamy, and the bacon adds richness.

Prep Time: 5 minutes
Cook Time: 6-8 hours
Servings: 4-6

Ingredients:
- 2 lbs. sweet potatoes, peeled, halved, and sliced
- 6 thick rashers all natural bacon
- 1 onion, finely diced
- 5 cloves garlic, minced
- 1 tsp ras el hanout *
- ½ tbsp. salt
- ¼ tsp ground black pepper
- ¼ tsp cayenne pepper
- 5 cups bone broth
- Chives, chopped (garnish)

Method:
1. Peel, half, and slice the sweet potatoes.
2. Cook half the bacon until crispy, and put aside to cool to make bacon crumbles.
3. Chop the uncooked bacon rashers into ¼ inch strips.
4. Pour the grease from the cooked bacon into the slow cooker, and add the uncooked bacon and all other ingredients.
5. Stir, then cover and cook on low for 6-8 hours.
6. Remove the cover and carefully blend the soup with a hand blender until it is smooth and even in consistency.
7. Serve with a garnish of bacon crumbles and chopped chives.

Ras-el-Hanout is a North African spice mixture that contains paprika, ginger, black pepper, cinnamon, coriander, cayenne pepper, and other spices. If you can't find it in your local stores you can make a simple version yourself by mixing equal parts paprika, ground coriander, and ginger. And if you're really stuck, just ground coriander will work!

Beef Soup

Tender beef shanks and sweet onions make this dish incredibly flavorful. The best bit? You're using the cheapest cut of beef in the grocery store!

Prep Time: 15 minutes
Cook Time: 6 hours + 8 hours
Servings: 4-6

Ingredients:
- 3 tbsp. lard or suet
- 4 sweet onions, coarsely chopped
- 2-3 beef shanks (cut approximately 2 inches thick)
- 1 tbsp. mustard powder (optional)
- Salt and pepper, to taste
- 4 pints bone broth (plus water to thin if necessary)

Method:
1. Place 2 tbsps. fat and onions in the slow cooker and cover.
2. Cook on low for 6 hours, or until caramelized (rich, caramel brown color) *.
3. While the onions are cooking, prepare the beef shanks by drying them and seasoning with salt, pepper, and mustard powder if desired.
4. Heat the remaining tbsp. of fat in a skillet and sauté the beef shanks for about 5-6 minutes per side, or until they are well-browned.
5. Carefully place the beef shanks on top of the caramelized onions in your slow cooker.
6. Add the bone broth and cover. Cook on low for another 8 hours.
7. Remove the beef shanks and chop the beef from the bone, and remove the marrow.
8. Return the chopped meat and marrow to the soup, stir and serve.

Caramelized onions are delicious in their own right, so you can make extra here and put some aside in the fridge to serve as a topping, or as a side with another meal. I love them on sausages!

Sides

Sagwala

Saag is a popular Indian dish that directly translates to 'pureed greens,' but the mixture of peppers, garlic and fragrant spices makes this taste nothing like bland baby food. I like to use mixture of spinach and mustard greens, but really any leafy green can be used for sagwala, even broccoli. This recipe calls for some specific Indian spices, but most are fairly common and can be found in your local stores or online.

Prep Time: 5 minutes
Cook Time: 4-6 hours
Servings: 4-6

Ingredients:
- 1 lb. spinach, washed and chopped into small pieces
- 1 lb. mustard leaves, washed and chopped into small pieces
- 1 sweet onion, peeled and diced
- 1 garlic pod (approx. 7-8 cloves), peeled and minced
- 1 jalapeno pepper, seeded and deveined, diced minced
- 2-inch stem fresh ginger, peeled and minced
- 1 tsp coriander
- 1 tsp cumin
- 1 tsp garam masala *
- ½ tsp turmeric
- ½ tsp cayenne pepper
- ½ tsp black pepper
- Pinch fenugreek
- 2 cups coconut milk
- 3 tbsp. ghee, preferably from pasture-raised, organic cattle

Method:
1. Put vegetables, spices, and coconut milk into the slow cooker, along with 2 tbsp. of ghee.
2. Cover and cook on low for 4 – 6 hours, or until greens have cooked down into a smooth consistency.
3. Serve with a small knob of ghee on top.

*If you can't find garam masala in your area, substitute equal amounts of allspice and cumin.

Cauliflower Risotto

Missing rice? This recipe makes a convincing risotto, but is 100% whole food compliant!

Prep Time: 5 minutes
Cook Time: 3 hours + 30 mins
Servings: 4-6

Ingredients:
- 2 cauliflower heads, washed and riced
- 2 cloves garlic, minced
- 1 ½ cups broth (vegetable, chicken or bone)
- Salt and pepper, to taste
- 1 cup fresh green peas, shelled
- 2 cups mushrooms, stemmed and diced (optional)

Method:
1. Place cauliflower, garlic, broth and seasonings into the slow cooker and stir.
2. Cover and cook on high for 3 hours (The cauliflower is now cooked).
3. Remove the lid and add the peas and mushrooms.
4. Change the setting to low, and cook for another 30 minutes.
5. Serve hot.

Bacon Brussels

Prep Time: 5 minutes
Cook Time: 3 hours + 5 mins
Servings: 4-6

Ingredients:

- 1 lb. fresh Brussel sprouts, cleaned
- 4 rashers all-natural bacon
- 1 tbsp. lard + bacon grease
- 1 fresh lime, juiced
- Pepper and salt, to taste

Method:

1. Prepare Brussel sprouts by washing in fresh water, and removing old outer leaves and woody stem. Cut an X in the base with a knife.
2. Cook the bacon in a skillet on the stove top until crispy. Remove cooked rashers from the skillet and set aside to cool. Carefully drain the bacon grease from the skillet into the crockpot.
3. Place lard, lime juice and seasonings in the slow cooker, and add Brussel sprouts. Stir until sprouts are coated with fat and seasoning mixture.
4. Crumble the bacon on top.
5. Cover and cook on high for 2-3 hours. You want the Brussel sprouts to be cooked, but not mushy.

Ratatouille

This classic French dish can be served as a hearty side with fish or meat, alone as a simple supper, or for a light vegetarian entrée.

Prep Time: 10 minutes
Cook Time: 6 hours
Servings: 2-4

Ingredients:
- 6 tbsp. olive oil
- 1 eggplant, cubed
- 1 yellow onion, peeled and diced
- 3 cloves garlic, minced
- 1 zucchini, cubed
- 3 ½ cups tomatoes, diced
- ½ green bell pepper, seeded and diced
- ½ yellow bell pepper, seeded and diced
- 1 cup mushrooms, quartered
- 1 cup all-natural tomato juice
- Salt and pepper, to taste
- 1 fresh bouquet garni *

If you do not have access to fresh herbs for a bouquet garni substitute 1 tsp dried thyme, ¼ cup chopped parsley, and a bay leaf.

Method:
1. Heat 2 tbsp. olive oil in a skillet and brown the eggplant and onion.
2. When the onion is translucent, add the garlic and sauté for another 1-2 minutes. Add more olive oil if necessary.
3. Put the eggplant, onion, garlic mixture into the slow cooker and add the remaining vegetables, tomato juice, and olive oil.
4. Season with salt and pepper, and add the bouquet garni or dried herbs.
5. Cook on low for 4-6 hours.
6. Remove the bouquet garni and adjust seasonings to taste before serving.

Garlic Vegetable Mash

Combining a trio of vegetables with the traditional herbs 'parsley, sage, rosemary, and thyme' makes a great side or vegetarian entree. Top with a sprinkle of toasted sunflower seeds before serving to add texture.

Prep Time: 15 minutes
Cook Time: 6 hours
Servings: 4-6

Ingredients:
- 4 carrots, peeled and diced
- 1 head of cauliflower, chopped
- 1 head of broccoli, chopped
- 2 cloves garlic, minced
- 1 tbsp. fresh rosemary, diced
- 1 tbsp. dried sage
- 1 tbsp. dried thyme
- 1 tbsp. olive oil
- ½ cup parsley, chopped
- Salt and pepper, to taste
- 4 cups chicken or vegetable broth

Method:
1. Prepare all ingredients as in the list above, and put vegetables and seasonings except parsley, and broth in the slow cooker.
2. Stir to mix.
3. Cover and cook on low for 6 hours, or high for 3 hours.
4. Once cooked, drain any excess liquid from the vegetable mixture and add the olive oil and parsley.
5. Mash by hand for a coarse texture, or blend with a hand blender to make a smooth creamier mix.
6. Adjust salt and pepper to taste.
7. Serve topped with a sprinkle of toasted sunflower seeds.

Entrees

The slow cooker makes main dish preparation easy. Most of these dishes can be started in the morning and left to cook through the day so that they are ready to serve for dinner. This chapter is separated into four sections according to recipe. Meat dishes are beef, pork, lamb, and game, poultry is chicken, turkey, duck and other birds. The seafood section has fish dishes, and then there is a vegetarian section for people who prefer to eat an animal-free diet.

Meat Dishes

Shepherd's Pie

The name of this dish comes from the ground lamb meat that is the main ingredient, but you can easily substitute any kind of ground meat – beef, turkey, or pork.

Prep Time: 5 minutes
Cook Time: 4 hours
Servings: 4

Ingredients (For Pie):
- 1 lb. pasture-raised lamb, ground
- 1 yellow onion, diced
- 6-10 green beans, chopped
- 3 carrots, peeled and diced
- 1 cup tomatoes, diced
- ⅓ cup bone broth
- 2 cloves garlic, minced
- 1 tbsp. nutritional yeast
- 1 tsp thyme
- Salt and pepper, to taste

Ingredients (Toppings):
- 2 lbs. potatoes, peeled and diced
- 2 tbsp. ghee
- 2 tbsp. coconut milk
- Salt and pepper, to taste

Method:
1. In a medium skillet, brown ground lamb.
2. Drain grease, and put into the slow cooker.
3. Add onion, green beans, carrots, tomatoes, bone broth, garlic, nutritional yeast, and thyme.
4. Season with salt and pepper, and stir to mix.
5. Cover and cook on low for 6-8 hours.
6. While the pie ingredients are cooking, boil the potatoes in salted water for 20 minutes or until soft.
7. Drain water and mash with 1 tbsp. ghee, coconut milk, salt and pepper.
8. Put the meat filling into a large oven-safe baking dish.
9. Carefully layer the mashed potato on top of the meat, and dot with small pats of ghee.
10. Broil until the ghee is melted and the potatoes start to brown.

Tacos Carnitas

Carnitas are traditionally served with fresh corn tortillas, a sprinkle of chopped onion and cilantro, and a squeeze of lime. So making them whole food compliant is as easy as replacing the tortilla with a large romaine lettuce leaf. Vary your spice level by adjusting the amount of serrano peppers you use, and if you really like the heat dice up some extra and throw them on top of your taco. Delicioso!

Prep Time: 10 minutes
Cook Time: 4-6 hours
Servings: 4-6

Ingredients:
- 1 tbsp. chili powder
- 1 tsp ground cumin
- Salt and pepper, to taste
- 3 lbs. boneless pork shoulder, rinsed and dried
- 1 tbsp. lard or suet
- 1 bunch (4-6) fresh whole shallot onions with stems, washed
- 2-4 serrano peppers, sliced in half lengthways (add more to increase the spice)
- 4 tbsp. lime juice, fresh squeezed if possible
- 8-12 large romaine leaves, washed

Optional Toppings:
- ¼ cup red onion, finely diced
- ¼ cup fresh cilantro, chopped
- ¼ cup serrano peppers, seeded and finely diced
- 1 lime, cut into small squeezable pieces
- Fresh guacamole (mashed avocado, lime juice and salt)

Method:
1. Make a dry rub with the chili powder, cumin, salt and pepper.
2. Coat the pork with the fat, then pat the spices onto it, rubbing gently so that the meat is evenly coated with fat and spices.
3. Place the seasoned meat, whole onions and serrano peppers into the slow cooker.
4. Add the lime juice and cover.
5. Cook on low for 4-6 hours, or until the pork easily shreds with a fork.
6. Remove the pork, and shred it completely. Remove any chunks of fat, and mix the shredded meat back into the juices in the slow cooker.
7. Serve with romaine lettuce 'tacos' and toppings as desired.

Rabbit Hotpot

This recipe reminds me of my grandmother who kept rabbits in her yard, not as pets, but as a source of fresh and economical meat for her large family. Not many people keep rabbits for food these days, but they are an excellent low fat, low cholesterol meat with a delicious nutty flavor. Ask your local butcher for fresh rabbit, or shop online for frozen meat.

Prep Time: 10 minutes
Cook Time: 6 hours
Servings: 2-4

Ingredients:
- 1 prepared rabbit
- ½ tsp ground black pepper
- 5 rashers all-natural bacon
- ¼ cup arrowroot or tapioca flour
- 2 cups bone broth or other stock
- 2 onions, peeled and chopped
- 2 cups tomatoes, diced
- 1 cup mushrooms, diced
- 2 carrots, peeled and sliced
- 2 potatoes, peeled and quartered (optional)
- 3 stalks celery, chopped
- 1 tbsp. balsamic vinegar
- 2 bay leaves, fresh if possible
- 1 tsp oregano

Method:
1. Place the rabbit in the slow cooker and season it with ground black pepper.
2. Lay the bacon rashers over the rabbit.
3. In a large bowl, whisk the arrowroot or tapioca flour into the stock, then add all other ingredients and stir to combine.
4. Pour the mixture over the rabbit.
5. Cover and cook on low for 6-8 hours, depending on the size of your rabbit.
6. When cooked, turn the slow cooker off and let the rabbit sit in the juice for 30 more minutes.

7. Scoop the rabbit out and place on a serving platter. It should cut easily, or can even be torn by hand into chunks for serving.
8. Eat your rabbit with the vegetables and juices from the pot.

Note: Rabbit bones can be quite small and sharp, so be careful as you eat.

Traditional Beef Stew

Prep Time: 10 minutes
Cook Time: 6-8 hours
Servings: 4-6

Ingredients:

- 1 ½ cups onion, diced
- 3 carrots, peeled and sliced
- 2 potatoes, peeled and quartered (optional)
- 1 celery stalk, chopped
- 1 lb. beef stew meat, cubed
- 1 red bell pepper, seeded and chopped
- 1 cup tomatoes, diced
- 2 tsp fresh thyme, diced
- 2 bay leaves, fresh if possible
- 3-inch whole sprig fresh rosemary, or 2 tsp dried
- Salt and pepper, to taste
- 2 cups bone broth or other stock
- ¼ cup arrowroot or tapioca flour

Method:

1. Put the onions, carrots, potatoes and celery in the bottom of the slow cooker.
2. Add the meat cubes on top.
3. Place the bell pepper, tomatoes and herbs on top of the meat and season to taste with salt and pepper.
4. Lastly, whisk the arrowroot or tapioca flour into the bone broth and pour the liquid into the slow cooker.
5. Cover and cook on low for 6-8 hours or overnight.
6. Serve hot.

Caribbean Beef Stew

If you're not a fan of traditional beef stew, you might prefer this tropical twist on the recipe that includes plantains, collard greens, and allspice. Try this recipe with lamb or chicken for a different taste.

Prep Time: 10 minutes
Cook Time: 6-8 hours
Servings: 4-6

Ingredients:
- 3 cups collard greens, washed and chopped
- 3 plantains, peeled and sliced thickly
- 1½ lb. beef stew meat, cubed
- 3 cloves garlic, minced
- 3 tbsp. smoked paprika
- 1 tbsp. allspice *
- 1 tsp. chili powder
- 2 whole dried red chili peppers
- Salt, to taste
- 3 cups chicken stock, or water

*Allspice is easily substituted by equal measures of cloves, cinnamon, and nutmeg.

Method:
1. Layer the ingredients in the bottom of the slow cooker, starting with collard greens, then sliced plantains, meat cubes, and lastly the spices.
2. Gently pour the stock into the pot, and cover.
3. Cover and cook on low for 6-8 hours or overnight.
4. Remove the whole chili peppers and serve.

Beef Pot Roast

Another traditional favorite. It might look like you slaved over a hot stove, but this is actually an easy recipe with very little clean-up. Throw in your favorite veggies around the meat and it's an elegant meal for a Sunday dinner or to impress guests. Left-overs can be used with salads or wrapped in lettuce leaves with a smear of yellow mustard as a quick snack or lunch to-go.

Prep Time: 10 minutes
Cook Time: 6-8 hours
Servings: 4-6

Ingredients:
- ¼ cup fresh parsley, minced
- ¼ cup fresh thyme, chopped
- 2 garlic cloves, peeled and minced
- 1/4 cup olive oil
- 2 tbsp. balsamic vinegar
- Salt and pepper, to taste
- 1 ½ - 2 lb. whole roast beef, rinsed and dried
- 1/2 cup bone broth or other stock
- 2-inch sprig whole fresh rosemary

Optional*:
- 6-8 small red potatoes
- 8-10 baby carrots
- 4-6 whole shallots

Method:
1. Mix the parsley, thyme, garlic, olive oil, vinegar and salt and pepper, and rub it over the beef to evenly coat it.
2. Pour the stock in to the slow cooker, and carefully place the beef into it.
3. Place the rosemary sprig in the liquid, along with small red potatoes, whole shallot onions, and baby carrots if desired. *
4. Cover and cook on low for 6-8 hours, or overnight.
5. Remove the vegetables and switch off the slow cooker.
6. Let the roast sit in the juices another 5 to 10 minutes before removing to serve.

Make sure you do not add more vegetables than what can comfortably fit in your slow cooker. All ingredients should be surrounded by liquid, and the beef should not touch the edges of the cooker pan.

Crock-Pot Cabbage Rolls

Prep Time: 15 minutes
Cook Time: 3 hours
Servings: 6

Ingredients:
- 1 green cabbage
- ½ lb. ground pork
- ½ lb. ground beef
- 1 small head cauliflower, washed and riced
- 1 sweet onion, diced
- ½ tsp oregano
- ½ tsp marjoram
- ½ tsp anise powder
- Salt and pepper, to taste
- 3 cups tomatoes, diced
- Toothpicks to hold the cabbage closed (optional)

Method:
1. Carefully separate the leaves from the cabbage head, wash, and set to dry on a clean dish cloth.
2. Put meats, riced cauliflower, onion and herbs and spices in a large mixing bowl and with clean dry hands, blend the mixture together so that all ingredients are evenly distributed.
3. Place 2 cups of diced tomatoes in a layer on the base of the slow cooker.
4. Take a golf-ball sized ball of the meat-veggie mixture and place in a dry cabbage leaf, rolling the leaf around it. You can secure it closed with a toothpick if you think it is necessary.
5. Place the cabbage roll seam side down on top of the tomatoes in the slow cooker.
6. Repeat until you run out of meat mixture, or the base of your slow cooker is filled.
7. Scatter the last cup of diced tomatoes on top of the cabbage rolls.
8. Cover and cook on high for 2-3 hours.
9. Serve hot with a spoon of the cooked tomatoes poured on top as a sauce.

Slow Cooked Pork Chops

Prep Time: 15 minutes
Cook Time: 3 hours
Servings: 4

Ingredients:
- ¼ cup arrowroot or tapioca flour
- 2 tsp. mustard powder
- 1 tsp, garlic powder
- Salt and pepper, to taste
- 6 to 8 pork chops
- 1 tbsp. lard
- 1 ½ cup bone broth

Method:
1. Mix the dry ingredients in a flat baking tray or plate.
2. Lay the pork chops in the dry mix so that both sides are coated. Keep the remaining mix to one side for later.
3. Melt the lard in a skillet and fry the pork chops for 1-2 minutes per side so that they are lightly browned.
4. Place the pork chops into the slow cooker.
5. Whisk the remaining dry mix into the bone broth and pour over the pork chops.
6. Cook on high for 2-3 hours, or low for 6-8 hours.
7. Serve with a side of dish, such as cauliflower risotto.

Poultry Dishes

Thai Chicken Wings

These wings are a delicious and healthy alternative to traditional buffalo hot wings. Make them for dinner, or for snacking.

Prep Time: 5 minutes
Cook Time: 4-6 hours
Servings: Varies

Ingredients:
- Coconut oil
- 3 lbs. pasture-raised chicken wings, thawed
- ½ cup almond or cashew butter
- 2 tbsp. lime juice
- 2 tbsp. fish sauce
- ¼ cup coconut milk
- 1 tsp cumin
- 2-inch stem of fresh ginger, grated

Method:
1. Grease the base of the slow cooker with coconut oil.
2. Put all ingredients other than chicken wings in a medium bowl and mix well.
3. Drop the wings into the bowl one by one, taking them out and laying them evenly distributed on the base of the slow cooker.
4. Pour the remaining sauce over the wings.
5. Cover and cook on low for 4-6 hours or until the sauce has thickened.
6. Remove the wings and place on serving dish with the remaining sauce poured over them.

Note: If you prefer dry wings you can crisp the wings under the broiler for 5-10 minutes before serving and use the sauce for dipping.

Kale Chicken Stew

This super easy stew is a staple in my household. You can mix and match vegetables depending on what's in season or in your fridge. You can do potatoes instead of beets, sweet potatoes in place of the carrots, and add green beans, zucchini, spinach ... whatever you like!

Prep Time: 5 minutes
Cook Time: 4-6 hours
Servings: 2-4

Ingredients:
- Skinless boneless chicken thighs, cut into 1-inch cubes
- 2 bunches of kale, washed and chopped with stems removed
- 1 onion, coarsely chopped
- 2 large carrots, peeled and sliced
- 1 large beet, peeled and cubed
- 2 garlic cloves, minced
- 2 cups chicken broth
- 1 cup Roma tomatoes, diced
- 2 tbsp. balsamic vinegar
- 1 tsp mustard powder
- 3 bay leaves
- Salt and pepper, to taste

Method:
1. Throw all the ingredients in the slow cooker and stir.
2. Cover and cook on high for 4-6 hours.
3. Taste and refine seasonings by adding more salt and pepper if needed.

Note: You can fix over-seasoning by adding a couple of potatoes to the pot when cooking. The potatoes will absorb the extra salt or spice etc. and can be removed before serving the stew.

Jamaican Jerk-Style Chicken

Take a trip to the tropics with the spicy-sweet flavors of this chicken. It's irie, mon!

Prep Time: 15 minutes
Cook Time: 5 hours
Servings: 4

Ingredients:

- 4 lbs. pasture-raised chicken thighs, bone-in and skin-on, rinsed
- 1 cup fresh pineapple, cubed (keep the juices)
- 8 green onions, finely chopped
- 2 habanero chilies, seeded and finely diced*
- 1–inch stem fresh ginger, peeled and grated
- 5 garlic cloves, peeled and minced
- ¼ cup fresh thyme, chopped
- 2 tsp ground allspice
- 1 tsp cinnamon powder
- 1/4 tsp cardamom
- 2-4 tbsp. lime juice
- Salt and pepper to taste
- Parchment paper

Be careful when preparing habanero peppers as they are very hot and the oil can stick to bare skin. Wear gloves, or wash your hands with vinegar after chopping peppers.

Method:

1. In a medium bowl mix all ingredients other than the chicken and diced pineapple.
2. Mash together until it is the consistency of a thick, spicy rub.
   Note: If you have a food processor or blender you can throw everything in and pulse to chop and mix the easy way.
3. Rub the chicken all over with the spice mixture, making sure it is evenly covered.
4. Line the base of the slow cooker with parchment paper and lay the chicken pieces on it.
5. Pour the pineapple cubes and juice over and around the chicken.
6. Cover and cook on low for 5 hours.
7. Remove and serve hot, with any remaining pineapple chunks on top.

Optional: If you prefer more crunchiness to your wings, after removing the chicken from the slow cooker you can brown it on a baking sheet in the broiler or a toaster oven until the skin is crisped.

Tikka Masala

Indian food is one of my favorite cuisines, and this chicken tikka masala is one of my family's favorite dishes. This version has very little spice, but you can up the heat factor by adding diced fresh serrano peppers or using hot curry paste instead of mild.

Prep Time: 5 minutes (slightly longer if skinning your tomatoes first)
Cook Time: 6-8 hours
Servings: 4-6

Ingredients:
- 3 lbs. boneless, skinless chicken thighs, rinsed
- 3 ½ cups tomatoes, skinned* and diced with juice retained
- 2 cups coconut milk
- 1 white onion, diced
- 4 garlic cloves, minced
- 1 tbsp. mild red curry paste
- 2 tbsp. garam marsala (or 1 tbsp. each cumin and allspice)
- 1½ tsp paprika
- Salt, to taste
- 1-4 serrano peppers, seeded and diced (optional)

*If using fresh tomatoes, I recommend skinning them for this dish. Dropping them into a pan of boiling, salted water until you see the skin split and wrinkle apart. (This should take approx. 30-seconds.) Allow to cool, and you will be able to easily remove the skin.

Method:
1. Place all the ingredients into the slow cooker and stir to mix.
2. Cover and cook for 6-8 hours or overnight.
3. Serve alone, or with a whole food side such as cauliflower rice, sautéed green beans, or boiled red potatoes.

Thai Chicken Curry

Another super easy dish, this is more of a Thai style green curry than the red Tikka Masala in the previous recipe. Again this is a mild version, so feel free to increase the spice by adding more chili peppers.

Prep Time: 5 minutes
Cook Time: 6-8 hours
Servings: 4-6

Ingredients:
- 2 ½ lbs. boneless skinless chicken breasts, cut into large chunks
- 3 cups coconut milk
- ½ cup chopped onion
- 2 cloves garlic, minced
- 1-inch stem fresh ginger, peeled and grated
- 1/2 tsp ground pepper
- 1 tsp cumin
- 1 tsp coriander
- 1 tsp turmeric
- 1 tsp paprika
- 3 tbsp. coconut oil
- Salt, to taste
- 1-4 serrano peppers, seeded and diced (optional)

Method:
1. Place all the ingredients into the slow cooker and stir to mix.
2. Cover and cook for 6-8 hours or overnight.
3. Serve alone, or with a whole food side such as zoodles or broccoli rice.

Greek Chicken

Greek food brings the delicious, healthy tastes of the Mediterranean into your diet. Cook this dish on a dreary winter's day to add a ray of sunshine or alfresco on a warm summer's night. Kali orexi!

Prep Time: 10 minutes
Cook Time: 6-8 hours
Servings: 4-6

Ingredients:

- 2 ½ lbs. boneless skinless chicken breasts, rinsed and diced into 1-inch cubes
- 6 red potatoes, halved
- 1 red bell pepper, stemmed, seeded and sliced*
- 1 yellow bell pepper, stemmed, seeded and sliced*
- 2 cloves garlic, minced
- ½ cup Kalamata olives, pitted and halved
- ½ cup sun dried tomatoes, chopped
- ½ cup sesame seeds, ground
- 1 tbsp. dried dill
- 1 tsp dried oregano
- 1 cup chicken stock
- Salt & pepper to taste
- 1 lemon, quartered
- Parsley, chopped

Method:

1. Place all the ingredients except parsley and lemon juice into the slow cooker and mix well.
2. Cover and cook for 6-8 hours or overnight.
3. Taste and adjust seasonings as desired.
4. Serve with a squeeze of lemon juice, and a sprinkle of chopped parsley on top.

If you would like to use roasted peppers they will add an extra flavor.

Yes! Lasagna

No grains? No dairy? You can still get your lasagna fix with this version of the classic Italian comfort food. Although this recipe is pasta and cheese free, it has the richness and satisfying texture of the original casserole. Yes! Lasagna for dinner tonight!

Prep Time: 15 minutes
Cook Time: 6-8 hours
Servings: 4-6

Ingredients:
- 1 yellow onion, diced
- 4 garlic cloves, minced
- 2 tbsp. olive oil
- 1 ½ lb. pasture-raised, organic turkey, ground
- ½ cup sun-dried tomatoes, diced
- 5 cups tomatoes, diced
- 1 tsp dried oregano
- 1 tsp dried basil
- Salt and pepper, to taste
- ¼ cup fresh oregano leaves
- ¼ cup fresh basil leaves
- ¼ cup fresh parsley, chopped
- 2 large eggplants, sliced thinly lengthwise
- 2 large zucchini, sliced thinly lengthwise
- 1 cup roasted red bell peppers, in thin strips *
- Nutritional yeast (optional)

*Use canned roasted red bell peppers, or cut roast halved peppers skin side up on a baking sheet at 450 F, or until the skin starts to wrinkle and bubble and is starting to burn slightly gently. Remove and cut into thin strips, then marinate in a sealed container with a tsp. each of olive oil and balsamic vinegar until ready to use.

Method:

1. Sauté the onion and garlic in olive oil on low heat until the onion turns translucent.
2. Add the ground turkey and raise the heat slightly. Cook, stirring frequently, until the meat is browned.
3. Add sun-dried tomatoes and fresh tomatoes, stir and season with dried herbs, salt and pepper.
4. Cook on medium heat for 5 minutes or until the fresh tomatoes start to soften. This is your lasagna sauce.
5. Pour 1-2 cups of the sauce into your slow cooker, covering the bottom to a depth of at least ½ inch.
6. Sprinkle with fresh herbs and cover with strips of eggplant, then add more sauce and fresh herbs and cover with strips of zucchini.
7. Do the same for red pepper.
8. Continue until you run out of an ingredient or the slow cooker is full.
9. Finish with a layer of sauce and fresh herbs.
10. Cook on low for 4-6 hours.
11. Serve in bowls with a sprinkle of nutritional yeast, if desired.

Thai Style Turkey Meatballs

Prep Time: 10 minutes
Cook Time: 2 hours
Servings: 6

Ingredients:
- Coconut fat
- 3 cups cauliflower, riced
- 2 large eggs
- 1 ½ lb. pasture-raised organic turkey, ground
- 2 cups cashews or almonds, ground
- 1 cup sunflower seeds, ground
- 1 red onion, finely diced
- 2 garlic cloves, minced
- 2-inch stem of fresh ginger, peeled and thinly sliced
- ¼ tsp red pepper flakes
- ½ tsp coriander
- ½ tsp cumin
- ½ tsp curry powder
- Salt and pepper, to taste
- 2 cups coconut milk
- 1 lime, sliced
- Fresh cilantro springs (garnish)

Method:
1. Grease the inside of your slow cooker with the coconut fat and evenly spread the riced cauliflower on the bottom.
2. Beat the egg and mix in all ingredients other than the coconut milk and lime slices.
3. Press meat mixture into walnut-sized balls and place on top of the cauliflower.
4. Place a slice of lime on the top of each patty, and scatter any remainder into the slow cooker.
5. Pour the coconut milk over and around the patties and cauliflower.
6. Cover and cook on high for 3 hours.
7. Scoop the meat balls out and serve over the riced cauliflower, topped with a sprig of fresh cilantro.

Seafood Dishes

Seafood is a healthy and nutritional way to add protein to your diet, However, with the problem of over-fishing and damage to the environment from some intensive shrimp farming methods it is important to always know where your seafood comes from and how it was caught. Only buy your seafood from markets where the origin and catch method are clearly marked or from vendors that are knowledgeable about sustainable fishing practices. The seafoodwatch.org site has an excellent website that maintains an up to date list of sustainable seafood.

Slow Cooked Shrimp 'Fettuccini'

This is a fast and easy dish for date night or anytime you want a romantic or celebration dinner. I recommend serving this rich and garlicky shrimp on a bed of sautéed eggplant noodles to add to the special occasion atmosphere.

Prep Time: 6 minutes
Cook Time: 1 ½ hours
Servings: 2-3

Ingredients:
- 1 lb. 16/20 count raw shrimp, rinsed, peeled and deveined
- 1 cup chicken broth
- 1 cup light coconut milk
- 3 tbsp. olive oil
- 2 cloves garlic, minced
- 2 tbsp. parsley
- ½ tsp red pepper flakes, optional
- ½ lemon, juiced
- Salt and pepper to taste
- 1/4 cup fresh basil leaves, shredded (garnish)
- ½ lemon, sliced (garnish)

For the Noodles:
- 1 large eggplant, peeled and cut into long thin noodle-like strips
- 2 tbsp. olive oil

Method:
1. Put everything except the fresh basil and lemon slices into your slow cooker.
Note: If you have the shrimp shells, put them into a muslin bag or sealed strainer and add to the slow cooker for extra richness to the sauce.
2. Cover and cook on high for 1 ½ hours.
3. Just before the shrimp is done, heat olive oil in a skillet to make your eggplant noodles.
4. When the oil is hot, toss the eggplant noodles in and sauté over a medium heat for 5 minutes or until softened and lightly browned. Stir frequently.
5. Serve shrimp and sauce over a bed of noodles, garnished with the fresh basil and a lemon slice.

Salmon Fillets

A classic fish dish made simple! Parchment paper is the secret here to keep the salmon moist during cooking.

Prep Time: 15 minutes
Cook Time: 1 ½ - 2 hours
Servings: 4-6

Ingredients:
- 1 bunch spring onions or shallots, washed and halved lengthways
- 4 sticks celery, washed and cut into 3-inch lengths (keep leaves)
- 1 spring fresh fennel, optional
- 1 ½ cups fish or chicken stock
- 1 lb. skin-on salmon fillets
- ½ cup ghee
- 1 lemon, sliced
- ½ cup capers
- Salt and pepper, to taste
- Parchment paper squares

Method:
1. Line the slow cooker with a large piece of parchment paper, you want it large enough that you will be able to fold it down over the salmon once it is inside the slow cooker.
2. Place the spring onions, celery and fennel to form a layer on the bottom of the slow cooker and cover with the stock.
3. Prepare the salmon by cutting into individual serving sizes.
4. Place the salmon pieces skin-side down on top of the vegetable layer and top each piece with a small knob of ghee, slice of lemon, capers and salt and pepper to taste. Do not layer more than two salmon pieces deep.
5. Fold the edges of the parchment paper down to cover the salmon, this will help keep juice and steam from the stock from evaporating.
6. Cover the slow cooker and set to cook on low for 1 ½ hours.
7. Carefully lift the lid (watch for steam!) and check to see if the salmon is done. It will be an opaque pink and will flake with a fork when fully cooked.
8. If not cooked, set on low and cook for another half hour.
9. Serve the salmon fillets hot with the aromatic vegetables from the base of the cooker on the side, or put in an airtight container in the fridge and serve cold with a green salad.

Seafood Chowder

This is a whole food dish based on the traditional New England fish chowder. It's perfect piping hot on a rainy afternoon. I like mine served with a dash of tabasco for spice. Yum!

Prep Time: 15 minutes
Cook Time: 1 ½ - 2 hours
Servings: 4-6

Ingredients:

- 4 rashers bacon
- 1 ½ lb. tilapia fillets (or other sustainable white fish), rinsed and cut into 1-inch cubes
- 2 cups fish stock, chicken broth, or a combination
- 5 red potatoes, washed and halved
- 1 small yellow squash, diced into ½-inch cubes
- 1 small zucchini, diced into ½-inch cubes
- 1 small white onion, peeled and diced small
- 1 large or 2 small carrots, peeled and sliced
- 1 stick of celery, sliced approx. ¼ inch thick
- 2 cloves garlic, minced
- 1 tsp dried tarragon
- 1 bay leaf, fresh if possible
- Salt and pepper ,to taste
- 2 cups whole-fat coconut milk
- Sprigs of fresh parsley (garnish)

Method:

1. Cook bacon in a skillet until crispy. Set aside to cool, and drain fat into the slow cooker.
2. Crumble bacon into slow cooker, and add all other ingredients except coconut milk.
3. Stir and cover.
4. Cook on low for 10 hours.
5. Remove bay leaves and stir in coconut milk.
6. If you prefer a creamier soup, remove half and blend, then re-combine. Otherwise serve as is.
7. Add a sprig of parsley for garnish, and a dash of Tabasco if you like.

Veracruzana Snapper

Fresh caught red snapper from the Gulf of Mexico is delicious when cooked in the unique Mexico-meets-the Caribbean style of Veracruz.

Prep Time: 10 minutes
Cook Time: 6-8 hours + 20-30 minutes
Servings: 4-6

Ingredients:

- 1 ½ lbs. red snapper fillets, cut into 2-inch wide servings.
- ½ lemon, juiced
- 1 tbsp. olive oil
- ¼ cup fresh oregano leaves, finely chopped
- Pinch cinnamon
- ¼ cup capers
- Pinch cloves
- Salt and pepper, to taste
- 1 ½ cups fish stock
- 1 red onion, peeled and sliced into rings
- 3 garlic cloves, minced
- 1 -4 serrano peppers, finely chopped
- ½ cup green olives, thinly sliced
- 3 cups tomatoes, diced
- 3 ears of corn, cleaned and halved
- ½ lemon, sliced (to garnish)
- Sprigs of fresh cilantro (to garnish)

Method:

1. Rinse and pat dry the snapper fillets and place in a container with sealable lid.
2. Mix lemon juice, olive oil, oregano, cinnamon, capers, cloves, salt and pepper to make a marinade.
3. Pour marinade over the snapper fillets, seal the container and set aside in the fridge.
4. Put the fish stock, onion, garlic, serrano peppers, olives, tomatoes and ears of corn into the slow cooker.

Note: Adjust the heat of this dish by varying the amount of serrano peppers you use. If you prefer no spice, you can omit the peppers altogether or substitute ½ cup diced bell pepper.

5. Cover and cook on low for 6-8 hours.
6. Remove the ears of corn and set aside.
7. Add the marinated fish and any remaining marinade to the slow cooker.
8. Cover and cook on high for 20 – 30 minutes.
9. Serve garnished with fresh cilantro and lemon slices, with the corn on the side.

Pescado Braziliano

This colorful South American fish stew melds coconut milk, lime juice and paprika to make a flavorful sauce. Although made in a similar manner to the Veracruzana snapper in the previous recipe, this thick stew has a very different taste.

Prep Time: 10 minutes
Cook Time: 6-8 hours + 20-30 minutes
Servings: 4-6

Ingredients:

- 4 tbsp. lime juice
- 1 tbsp. coriander
- 1 ½ tbsp. paprika
- Salt and pepper, to taste
- 2 lbs. tilapia fillets (or other sustainable white fish), rinsed and cut into 1-inch cubes
- 1 red bell pepper, seeded and cut into strips
- 1 yellow or orange bell pepper, seeded and cut into strips
- 1 green bell pepper, seeded and cut into strips
- 1 large onion, chopped
- 3 cloves garlic, mined
- 1 lime, sliced
- 1 cup fish stock
- 1 cup coconut milk
- 2 Roma tomatoes, chopped
- ½ cup fresh cilantro, chopped (to garnish)

Method:

1. Mix lime juice, coriander, paprika, salt, and pepper in a sealable container, add the cubed fish and stir to coat. Seal the container and set aside in the fridge.
2. Put the bell peppers, onion, garlic, sliced lime, fish stock, and coconut milk into the slow cooker.
3. Cover and cook on low for 6-8 hours.
4. Remove the lime slices, and add the marinated fish and diced tomatoes to the slow cooker.
5. Cover and cook on high for 20 – 30 minutes.
6. Serve garnished with fresh cilantro.

Vegetarian Dishes

All Veggie Chili

This veggie chili is best made with fresh winter vegetables. While potatoes and carrots are basic, you can add rutabaga, Brussel sprouts, kale, turnips, winter squash or any other vegetables you like.

Prep Time: 10 minutes
Cook Time: 6-8 hours
Servings: 6-8

Ingredients:
- 6 small red potatoes, halved
- 4 carrots, peeled and diced
- 1 parsnip, peeled and diced
- 1 beet, peeled and diced
- 3 cups tomatoes, diced
- 1 yellow onion, diced
- 2 garlic cloves, minced
- 1 cup vegetable broth
- 1 tbsp. chili powder
- 1 tbsp. paprika
- 1 tbsp. cumin
- 1 tbsp. nutritional yeast (optional)
- 2 tsp dried oregano
- 1 tsp red pepper flakes
- 1 tsp cayenne pepper
- ½ tsp sea salt
- Several sprigs chopped parsley, to garnish (optional)

Instructions:
1. Prepare all ingredients as in the list above, and put into the slow cooker.
2. Cover and cook on low for 6-8 hours.
3. Serve with springs of parsley for garnish.

Tortilla de Patatas

Although it's known in English as a Spanish omelet, this versatile dish is more of a thick egg pie than what we normally consider an omelet. It's categorized here as an entree, but it is great for just about any meal: Eat it warm straight from the cooker (try it with a side of ratatouille); pack a slice for a cold lunch with a simple side salad of cucumber and cherry tomatoes drizzled with olive oil; or eat it either cold or warmed in a little olive oil on a low heat for a fast and nutritious breakfast.

Prep time: 15 mins
Cook time: 2 hours
Serves: 2-4

Ingredients:
- 1 tbsp. olive oil
- 2 cups potato, diced into very small cubes or thinly sliced (your preference) *
- 1 cup yellow onion, diced
- 1 cup red bell pepper, diced**
- 1 tbsp. coconut oil
- 8 large eggs
- Salt and pepper, to taste
- 2 tbsp. chopped fresh parsley (optional)
- 2 tbsp. drained capers (optional)

*Regular potatoes are considered a whole food, but you can use sweet potatoes (yams) if you prefer.
**Red bell pepper is traditional, but any color is fine. I like to use a mixture.

Method:
1. Prep vegetables, and lightly sauté in olive oil at low heat until onion is clear and potato is starting to brown.
2. Coat the inside of your slow cooker with coconut oil and add the hot vegetable mixture straight from the skillet.
3. Whisk eggs and season with salt and pepper to taste.
4. Pour eggs over the vegetables. Do not stir!
5. Cover and cook on low for 2 - 2 ½ hours, or until the eggs are completely set.
6. Allow the cooked tortilla to cool slightly, then tip onto a plate and serve with a sprinkle of chopped parsley and capers.

Zoodles Primavera

Prep time: 5 mins
Cook time: 3 hours
Serves: 4

Ingredients:
- 4 zucchini, spiralized to make zoodles
- 4 cups tomatoes, diced
- 2 tbsp. tomato paste
- 2 cups mushrooms, diced
- 1 cup broccoli, chopped
- ½ cup cauliflower, chopped
- 1 carrot, peeled and diced
- 1 red onion, peeled and diced
- ½ red bell pepper, seeded and diced
- 1 bunch fresh spinach, washed and chopped
- 3 garlic cloves, minced
- ¼ cup fresh basil, minced
- ¼ cup fresh oregano, minced
- ½ tsp dried sage
- ½ tsp dried thyme
- Small spring fresh rosemary
- 2 tbsp. olive oil
- Salt and pepper, to taste

Method:
1. Add everything except the zoodles into the slow cooker and stir well.
2. Cover and cook on low for 4 hours.
3. If desired, blend to make a smooth sauce.
4. Add zoodles and stir.
5. Cook on high for 30 minutes.

Stuffed Peppers

Replacing the meat with a rich pecan mixture makes these peppers 100% vegetarian, and tasty enough to satisfy even the most die-hard meat-lover. Try making these with poblano peppers for an interesting twist.

Prep time: 15 mins
Cook time: 4 hours
Serves: 4

Ingredients:
- 3 large green bell peppers, halved lengthwise and deseeded (do not remove stems).
- 1 cup Roma tomatoes, diced and drained
- 3 cups ground pecans
- ¼ cup white onion, very finely chopped
- 1 clove garlic, minced
- 1 tsp dried or fresh sage
- 1 tsp dried or fresh thyme
- 1 large egg, beaten
- 2 tbsp. coconut milk
- ¼ cup almond flour (optional)
- 1 tbsp. olive oil (to grease the pan)
- ½ cup vegetable stock or fresh water

Method:
1. Mix together all ingredients (except for bell pepper and stock) to form a stiff mixture that holds together.
2. If it's too dry, add a little extra coconut milk, if too wet, add a little almond flour.
3. Fill each pepper with the mixture. You should lightly push it down so that you fit as much as possible, but do not over-fill.
4. Lightly grease the inside of the slow cooker pan with olive oil, and lay the peppers inside.
5. Carefully pour the vegetable stock or water around the peppers (not over them).
6. Cover and cook on low for 4 hours.
7. Serve with a side of ratatouille, or on a bed of cauliflower risotto.

Vegetable Korma

This mild curry is a perfect way to spice up your vegetables. Creamy and satisfying, this naturally whole food compliant dish has been a vegetarian favorite for years. This recipe calls for sweet potatoes, carrots, and green beans, but feel free to use whatever you have on hand. Throw in some pineapple or pumpkin, and add a sprinkle of raisins. With this versatile dish you can mix and match vegetables to your heart's desire.

Prep time: 5 mins
Cook time: 8 hours
Serves: 4-6

Ingredients:
- 2 large sweet potatoes, peeled and diced
- 2 large carrots, peeled and diced
- 1 cup green beans, chopped
- ½ yellow onion, chopped
- 2 cloves garlic, minced
- 2-inch piece fresh ginger, peeled and grated
- 1 serrano pepper, seeded and diced
- 1 tsp ground cumin
- 1 tsp ground paprika
- ½ tsp chili powder
- ½ tsp ground turmeric powder
- ½ tsp Garam Masala
- ¼ tsp ground cardamom, ground
- 2 cups coconut milk
- 2 tsp almond flour
- ½ cup cashews, halved
- ¼ cup shredded coconut (optional for garnish)
- ¼ cup cilantro, chopped (optional for garnish)
- ¼ cup raisins (optional for garnish)

Method:
1. Put the prepared vegetables in the slow cooker.
2. Mix the spices, coconut milk and almond flour to make a paste.
3. Pour over the vegetables, coating them evenly. Stir.
4. Cover and cook on low for 8 hours.
5. The cooked korma should have a thick, creamy consistency; feel free to blend it if you don't like chunks.
6. Stir in the cashews.
7. Serve with chopped cilantro, shredded coconut, or even a few raisins on top.

Holiday Dinner Menu

The holidays are the easiest time of year to lose your resolve and break your diet. But there's no need for cheating when it's so easy to make delicious traditional recipes in your slow cooker. We've even included a festive spiced cider and pumpkin pie. Just follow the rules with these dishes, and there's no way you'll let the holidays stop you from winning the 30 Day Whole Food Slow Cooker Challenge!

Slow Roast Turkey and Gravy

Prep time: 15 mins
Cook time: 1 hour + 6-8 hours + 30 minutes
Serves: 6-8

Ingredients:
- 5 lb. pasture-raised, organic turkey breast
- 2 tsp ground sage
- 1 ½ tsp ground thyme
- 1 tsp ground marjoram
- ¾ tsp ground rosemary
- ½ tsp nutmeg
- ½ tsp finely ground black pepper
- 1 tbsp. ghee

For the Stuffing:
- 1 cooking apple
- 1 large garlic clove, peeled
- 2-3 whole cloves (optional)

For the Gravy:
- 2 cups chicken stock
- 1 cup water
- ½ tsp ground sage
- ½ tsp cumin
- 1 garlic clove, peeled and minced
- ½ tsp garlic salt
- 1 tsp garlic powder
- ½ cup arrowroot flour
- Salt and pepper, to taste

Method:

1. Core the apple and press garlic clove into it.
2. Rinse the turkey and pat dry.
3. Mix the spices and herbs with the ghee and rub into the turkey.
4. Place the turkey breast down in the slow cooker, and push the apple inside the breast cavity as far as you can.
5. Combine all the ingredients for the gravy and whisk or blend until smooth.
6. Pour the gravy mix around and inside the turkey.
7. Cover and cook on high for 1 hour, then on low for 6-8 hours.
8. Remove the turkey and place breast-side up in a roasting pan. Broil in a conventional oven for 30 minutes or until browned.
9. Pour the gravy into a small pitcher, or gravy boat if you have one.
10. Serve with all the trimmings!

Holiday Ham

What are the holidays without a sweet and juicy ham on the table? No worries that traditional recipes call for mountains of sugar or honey for a glaze, I solved that by dousing my ham in pineapple and OJ to add sweetness without the sugar!

Prep time: 15 mins
Cook time: 4-6 hours
Serves: 6-8

Ingredients:

- 4-5 lb. fresh natural ham
- 1 lemon, zested and juiced
- 1 orange, zested and juiced
- 1 tbsp. ground nutmeg
- 4 tbsp. lard
- 4-6 whole cloves (optional)
- 1 8 oz. can crushed pineapple in natural juice
- 1 tbsp. apple cider vinegar
- 1 sprig fresh rosemary
- 1 stick cinnamon

Method:

1. Rinse and dry ham, then score a diamond pattern in the top with a sharp knife to approximately ¼ inch deep.
2. Mix lemon zest, orange zest, nutmeg and lard and rub into the ham, making sure to get it into the cuts.
3. Press the cloves into the ham in a pattern, and place it into the slow cooker.
4. Mix the orange juice, lemon juice, pineapple, and apple cider vinegar and pour over the ham.
5. Drop the rosemary sprig and cinnamon stick into the liquid.
6. Cover and cook on low for 4-6 hours, basting with the juice occasionally.

Green Bean Casserole

Prep time: 10 mins
Cook time: 6 hours
Serves: 6-8

Ingredients:
- 8 rashers all natural thick cut bacon
- 1 white onion, chopped
- 2 cloves garlic, minced
- 1 ½ lbs. fresh string beans, ends trimmed
- ½ cup chicken stock
- Salt and pepper, to taste

Method:
1. Layer 4 rashers of bacon in a lattice pattern on the bottom of the slow cooker.
2. Cover with the onion, garlic and green beans.
3. Layer the remaining 4 rashers of bacon in a lattice pattern on top of the beans.
4. Pour the chicken stock over everything.
5. Cover and cook on low for 6 hours.
6. Stir before serving.

Cauliflower Mash

Although regular potatoes are considered whole foods, people watching their carb-intake may prefer to avoid them. I figured you probably knew how to make standard mash, so instead I've included this delicious potato-free low-carb alternative.

Prep time: 15 mins
Cook time: 2 hours
Serves: 4

Ingredients:
- 1 cauliflower head, cleaned and cut into florets
- 6 cloves garlic, peeled and coarsely chopped
- 1 cup vegetable broth
- 4-6 cups fresh water
- 3 tbsp. ghee
- 1 tbsp. fresh parsley, chopped
- 1 tbsp. fresh sage, chopped
- 1 tbsp. fresh rosemary, chopped
- 1 tbsp. fresh thyme, chopped
- Salt and pepper, to taste

Method:
1. Put cauliflower, garlic, and broth in the slow cooker.
2. Add enough water to cover, and cook on low heat for 6 hours
3. Drain the excess liquid and return the cauliflower and garlic cloves to the slow cooker.
4. Add the ghee and mash by hand or with a blender.
5. Stir in the fresh herbs, and season with salt and pepper to taste.
6. Serve warm.

Sweet Potato Pie

No Thanksgiving is complete without this quintessentially American dish, but you won't find any toasted marshmallows on this version. This pie contains only all-natural whole foods, with the sweetness coming from date paste.

Prep time: 10 mins
Cook time: 4 hours
Serves: 6-8

Ingredients:
- 2 eggs, beaten
- 1 tbsp. ghee
- 6 dates, pitted and mashed
- ½ cup coconut cream
- 2 tsp cinnamon
- 2 tsp natural vanilla powder
- Pinch of ground nutmeg
- 1 orange, zested and juiced
- Pinch of ground black pepper
- 3 lbs. sweet potatoes, peeled and cut into chunks
- 1 ½ cups chopped pecans, toasted

Method:
1. Mix together eggs, ghee, dates, coconut cream, cinnamon, vanilla, nutmeg, orange zest, and pepper until evenly combined in a thin paste.
2. Put a layer of sweet potato chunks to fill the bottom of the slow cooker.
3. Dab or drizzle about a third of the spice mixture evenly over the potatoes.
4. Add another layer of sweet potatoes, and again cover with the spice mixture.
5. Repeat for a third layer, and cover with the remaining spice mixture.
6. Cover and cook on low for 4 hours or until soft.
7. Gently mash the potatoes with a spoon. If they are dry, stir in the orange juice.
8. Serve in a shallow dish with toasted pecans scattered on top.

Pumpkin 'Pie'

This crustless 'pie' makes an excellent holiday dessert, but it's sugar free and healthy so you can enjoy it anytime - even for breakfast!

Prep time: 10 mins
Cook time: 2 hours + 15-30 minutes
Serves: 6-8

Ingredients:
- 1 tbsp. coconut butter or ghee
- 4 eggs, beaten
- 3 cups pumpkin puree
- 2 large, very ripe bananas, peeled and mashed
- 2 cups coconut cream
- 3 tbsp. almond butter
- Pumpkin pie spice, to taste
- ¾ cup pecans, toasted and chopped
- ½ cup shredded coconut

Method:
1. Grease the inside of your slow cooker with the coconut butter or ghee.
2. Blend together the eggs, pumpkin puree, bananas, coconut cream, almond butter, and pumpkin pie spice until evenly combined.
3. Pour into the slow cooker.
4. Cover and cook on low for 2 hours.
   Note: Trapping a paper towel under the lid of your slow cooker will absorb moisture and improve the consistency of the pumpkin as it cooks.
5. Remove the lid and scatter the pecans and shredded coconut over the top of the pumpkin.
6. Cover and cook for another 15-30 minutes, or until the pumpkin mixture is set and starts to pull away from the sides of the cooker.
7. Serve in bowls, or for a prettier presentation transfer the pumpkin to a serving dish before adding the pecans (while it is still slightly liquid) and bake in the oven for 30 minutes or until set.

Tropical Orange Spice Cider

Prep time: 5 mins
Cook time: 4 hours
Serves: 6-8

Ingredients:
- 6 sweet apples, cored & sliced
- 4 sweet oranges, peeled and sliced
- 6-8 cups fresh water
- 2 cinnamon sticks
- ½ cup dried hibiscus flowers (for tea)
- Additional orange slices and cinnamon sticks (optional as garnish)

Method:
1. Prep all ingredients as in the list above and put into the slow cooker, making sure there is plenty of liquid to cover the fruit.
2. Cover and cook on low for 5 hours.
3. Remove the lid and stir, mashing the apples and oranges into a pulp.
4. Cover and cook on high for another hour.
5. Strain the liquid through a mesh strainer to remove the pulp.
6. Return the liquid to the slow cooker and serve warm in mugs. Add a twist of orange and a cinnamon stick to the mug if desired.

No SWYPO Snacks

I know from personal experience that quitting sweets and processed foods can be as hard as giving up any other addiction. There will be times when your body is lying to you that you NEED sugar or junk food, right then and there, and these are the danger times when SWYPO foods beckon. But do not fear, fair whole foods champion, there is an alternative!

These foods may satisfy your sweet tooth, but they are definitely not in the SWYPO category. We're not recommending that you eat these all day, every day. Far from it - these foods are for use in emergency only. But there's no harm in keeping these recipes handy for when temptation strikes.

Sweet Fruit Sauce

Craving sugar? Try a spoonful – or a small bowl! – of this sweet and thick fruit sauce. Vary the fruit for different flavors; I like to make it tropical by using guavas instead of pears.

Prep time: 15 mins
Cook time: 2 hours
Serves: 4

Ingredients:
- 4 lbs. fresh apples and pears, washed and peeled
- 2 cups all-natural, organic, sugar-free dried fruit (e.g. apricots, mango, prunes, cranberries)
- 4 cinnamon sticks
- 1 cup fresh water

Method:
1. Prep all ingredients as in the list above and add to slow cooker.
2. Cover and cook for 4-6 hours, or until apples are tender and easy to mash.
3. Remove the cinnamon sticks and blend the sauce to an even, smooth consistency.
4. Cool and store in the fridge in air-tight containers.

Banana Not Bread

Okay, so this recipe is kinda SWYPO, but we won't tell if you don't!

Prep time: 5 mins
Cook time: 3-4 hours
Serves: 6

Ingredients:
- 1 tbsp. ghee
- 3 large extra ripe bananas, peeled and mashed
- 1 cup dates, pitted and mashed
- 2 cups almond or coconut flour
- 4 eggs, beaten
- 1 orange, zested (do not use juice)
- 1 tsp ground cinnamon
- ¼ tsp grated nutmeg

Method:
1. Grease the slow cooker with the ghee.
2. Prep all other ingredients as in the list above and blend together until the mixture has a smooth, even, creamy consistency.
3. Pour into the slow cooker.
4. Cover and cook on low for 3-4 hours or until the 'bread' is firm.
   Note: This is a good recipe to use the paper towel under the lid trick to absorb the excess moisture.
5. Tip out onto a plate and slice.

Stuffed Apples

These delicious apples don't need sugar to be completely decadent.

Prep time: 15 mins
Cook time: 2-4 hours
Serves: 4

Ingredients:

- 4 large crisp apples, half-cored with the bottom left closed
- ½ cup fresh water
- ½ cup coconut water
- ½ cup shredded coconut
- ½ cup raisins, quartered
- ¼ cup coconut butter
- ¼ cup almond butter
- 2 tbsp. cinnamon
- Pinch of grated nutmeg
- Pinch of salt
- Extra shredded coconut for topping (optional)

Method:

1. Prep the apples by taking out the top half of the core down to the seeds, but leaving the bottom so that the filling melds into the flesh of the apple rather than escaping out onto the baking dish. Scoop out a little extra to make a hollow to receive the stuffing, being careful not to get too close to the skin.
2. Combine the water and coconut water and pour into the slow cooker. Drop in the extra apple flesh you scooped out.
3. Mix the other ingredients together, and using a teaspoon carefully stuff the apples.
4. Carefully place the apples in the slow cooker, cover and cook on low for 2-4 hours or until the apple has the softness you prefer. Some like' em crispy, some like 'em mushy!
5. If these are for a dessert, you want to take them out of the slow cooker and serve with a sprinkle of coconut on top. But if they're just for you, you can dig right in with a spoon!

Steamy Plantains

Plantains are bananas tougher cousin, the bad fruit of the jungle! Unlike yellow-bellied bananas, plantains are at their best when they are spotted and deep brown.

Prep time: 2 mins
Cook time: 2 hours
Serves: 4-6

Ingredients:
- 4 ripe plantains
- 2 tbsp. ghee. melted
- coarse sea salt to taste
- 1-2 cups fresh water

Method:
1. Peel the plantains and slice lengthwise into long strips about ¼-inch thick.
2. Lay a raised rack on the base of your slow cooker, and add a small amount of water so you can steam the plantains. The rack must be above the level of the water on a greased.
3. Melt the ghee and brush onto both sides of each plantain slice, then lay on the rack.
4. Sprinkle sea salt over the plantains to taste.
5. Cook on low for 2 hours, making sure the water doesn't all evaporate.
6. Remove the plantains and serve hot.

Spicy Snack Almonds

Not all cravings are for sugar, and these spicy almonds will fill a late afternoon hollow belly perfectly. Keep these handy in your purse, your car, or your desk drawer for whenever hunger strikes.

Prep time: 5 mins
Cook time: 3 hours

Ingredients:

- 5 cups whole raw almonds
- 2 ½ tbsp. coconut oil
- 2 tsp garlic powder
- 1 tsp smoked paprika
- 1 tsp onion powder
- Salt and pepper, to taste

Method:

1. Cover the slow cooker and heat empty on high for approximately half an hour.
2. Add almonds and other ingredients, immediately stirring so that the almonds are evenly coated.
3. Cover and cook on low for 2 hours, stirring occasionally.
4. Remove the lid and cook uncovered on high, stirring frequently.
5. Serve warm immediately, or allow it to cool and store in an air-tight container.

Congratulations! What's Next?

You made it! You just completed the 30 Day Whole Food Slow Cooker Challenge, and I bet you're feeling great. Did you reach the three goals you set in Chapter Three? If you didn't, don't worry. There's still time, because even though your 30 days are up, your commitment to yourself and your health should be stronger than ever.

Are you going to go back to eating the old way – the unhealthy way? No way!

You no-longer have to eat 100% whole food compliant recipes, but you can't go crazy. David and Melissa Hartwig, creators of the original Whole Food 30-day Challenge, recommend that you slowly start to introduce foods back into your diet. Adding potential problem foods one by one means that you can pay attention to your body and notice when some of your old symptoms pop up.

What is most important is that we are all unique. Only you can tell what foods are best for you.

Are you ready to take it fast, or would you rather go slow?

There are two ways to start evaluating foods as you reintroduce them to your diet. The first, and in my opinion the easiest, is to take it slow. Choose this option is you are comfortable eating the whole food compliant diet most days. Then, on a special occasion or when the mood takes you, try a small amount of a non-whole food item and see what happens.

Drink a glass of wine and immediately bloat? Then you may need to limit or cut out alcohol from your diet. Chow down on chow mien from your local delivery service and get an unexpected headache on the side? Then MSG may be an issue for you.

Eventually you will just eat a 99.9% whole food diet naturally, indulging in off-track items only when you know it is really worth it for you and the rewards outweigh the negatives.

Taking the fast track.

If you are someone who wants to identify exactly what foods have negative effects on your health and well-being, then you can follow the schedule below to pinpoint your no-go items and clear others to reintroduce to your daily diet. I recommend keeping a daily diet diary where you write down what you ate and how you felt.

Day 1: Have a couple of drinks to celebrate!
You made it through the 30 Day Whole Food Slow Cooker Challenge, so toast your success with a glass or two of gluten-free alcohol such as red wine, hard apple cider, rum, or a shot of 100% agave tequila. Cheers!

Days 2 and 3: Whole foods only
Return to the whole food diet to evaluate what, if any, effect the alcohol had on your body.

Day 4: Time for legumes!
Dip apple slices in peanut butter, have a side of black beans with lunch, or a snack of hummus. Whatever your favorite legume is, from soy sauce to refried beans – go for it!

Days 5 and 6: Whole foods only
Again, return to the whole food diet and evaluate how your body feels. Are you tired, stomach gurgling? You now know what it is to have a clean, energetic and healthy body, so pay attention to anything that isn't tip-top and perfect.

Day 7: Non-gluten grains
Help yourself to rice! Or maybe you've been craving quinoa or oats or corn. Make yourself some chips and fresh salsa, or indulge in a big bowl of sugar-free granola.

Days 8 and 9: Whole foods only
Once more, go back to a strict whole food diet for two days to see how you feel.

Day 10: Dairy is allowed!
For one day let yourself eat cheese, plain yoghurt, milk and other dairy items. But remember to keep the rest of your diet 100% whole food compliant.

Days 11 and 12: Whole foods only
Return to the strict whole food diet for two days and monitor your body, energy levels, how you feel etc.

Day 13: Test out gluten
Day thirteen is appropriate to try foods containing the demonized gluten. Have a sandwich, or some crackers and almond butter, or a bowl of cereal with almond milk.

This is such a big one that you need to be careful not to slip and add in any other non-whole food compliant items. The aim is to only test foods that contain gluten, although you are finally allowed a cold beer!

Days 14 and 15:
Go back to a strict whole food diet for two days after your test day and see how eating gluten may have affected you.

Day 16: Sugar baby!

Don't go wild by mainlining Pixie Stix! Take it slow and easy, adding brown sugar to your coffee, having a little jam with your almond butter apple snack, or drizzling honey on your sweet potato. How does your body handle it?

Days 17 and 18:

Find out if sugar is okay for you by following a strict whole food diet for the last two days of your trial period to evaluate how your brush with sweetness has affected you.

Day 19 and onwards

By now you should have a pretty good idea of what foods your body can handle, and what you need to avoid. Keep experimenting with different foods or food combinations and never stop paying attention to your body and how what you eat is affecting you mentally and physically.

If you find your symptoms are creeping back, then return to a strict whole food diet for a few days, or until the symptoms subside.

Reaching your end goal.

You started the 30 Day Whole Food Slow Cooker Challenge because *you* wanted to feel better, be healthier, have more energy and be more mentally alert. You achieved that goal, but it was not the end. You have managed to break your bad eating habits, but now is the time for you to establish new ones!

The end goal of the 30 Day Whole Food Slow Cooker Challenge is not to keep to the recipes in this book for 30 days, but to find a new way of eating that is perfect for you. By completing the challenge and reintroducing foods, you have discovered the diet that matches your unique body. Keeping to this diet - *your diet* - is your end goal.

So relax. Pay attention to what your body is telling you, and eat what feels good. Crave the foods that nourish and energize you. Eat healthy. Eat whole. Eat happy.

Appendix

On the following pages you'll find printable forms and useful resources for the 30 days of your challenge and beyond.

Helpful Conversions

This book is written using conventional US cup measures, but you can use this guide to find equivalents for the metric and imperial systems.

Measurements & Equivalents:

Measurement	Equivalents		
a dash	8 drops (liquid)	≈ ⅛ tsp	
1 tsp	60 drops		
3 tsp	1 tbsp.	½ fl. oz.	
½ tbsp.	1½ tsp		
2 tbsp. (liquid)	1 fl. oz.	⅛ cup	
3 tbsp.	1 ½ fl. oz.	1 jigger	
4 tbsp.	¼ cup		
⅛ cup	2 tbsp.		
⅙ cup	2 tbsp. + 2 tsp		
⅓ cup	5 tbsp. + 1 tsp		
1 cup	½ pint	8 fl. oz.	
2 cups	1 pint	16 fl. oz.	
4 cups	1 quart	2 pints	32 fl. oz.
4 quarts	1 gallon		
1 peck	8 quarts	2 gallons	
1 bushel	4 pecks		

Volume Equivalents:

Metric	Imperial	US cups
250 ml.	8 fl. oz.	1 cup
180 ml.	6 fl. oz.	3/4 cup
150 ml.	5 fl. oz.	2/3 cup
120 ml.	4 fl. oz.	1/2 cup
75 ml.	2 1/2 fl. oz.	1/3 cup
60 ml.	2 fl. oz.	1/4 cup
30 ml..	1 fl. oz.	1/8 cup
15 ml.	1/2 fl. oz.	1 tbsp.

Teaspoons/Tablespoons to Milliliters		Tablespoons to US cups	
1 tsp	5 ml.	1 tbsp.	1/16 cup
2 tsp	10 ml.	2 tbsp.	1/8 cup
1 tbsp.	15 ml.	4 tbsp.	1/4 cup
2 tbsp.	30 ml.	5 tbsp.	1/3 cup
3 tbsp.	45 ml.	8 tbsp.	1/2 cup
4 tbsp.	60 ml.	10 tbsp.	2/3 cup
5 tbsp.	75 ml.	12 tbsp.	3/4 cup
6 tbsp.	90 ml.	16 tbsp.	1 cup
7 tbsp.	105 ml.	18 tbsp.	1 1/8 cups

Weight Equivalents:

Imperial	Metric	US Cups
½ oz.	15 g.	N/A
1 oz.	30 g.	N/A
2 oz.	60 g.	N/A
3 oz.	90 g.	N/A
4 oz.	110 g.	N/A
5 oz.	140 g.	N/A
6 oz.	170 g.	N/A
7 oz.	200 g.	N/A
8 oz.	225 g.	N/A
9 oz.	255 g.	N/A
10 oz.	280 g.	N/A
11 oz.	310 g.	N/A
12 oz.	340 g.	N/A
13 oz.	370 g.	N/A
14 oz.	400 g.	N/A
15 oz.	425 g.	N/A
1 lb.	450 g.	N/A

A Quick Whole Foods Yes/No Guide

30 Day Whole Food Slow Cooker Challenge Menu Planner

Week: _____

Day \ Meal	Monday	Tuesday	Wednesday	Thursday	Friday	Saturday	Sunday
Breakfast							
Lunch							
Snack							
Dinner							

I am taking this challenge because:

1. ➢ _____

2. ➢ _____

3. ➢ _____

99

Whole Foods

- Natural cuts of meat, preferably organic, grass-fed or naturally raised
- Naturally smoked or salt-cured meats
- Natural seafood, preferably from a sustainable source
- Eggs, preferable free-range
- Vegetables
- Fruit and unsweetened fruit juice.
- Nuts and seeds (in limited amounts)
- Fresh pod legumes. These are legumes eaten with their pod, such as snap peas and green beans
- Dried and fresh herbs, spices, and salt
- Black coffee and teas
- Vinegar
- Coconut in any form: butter, oil, milk, meat, dried or canned
- Animal fats, clarified butter or ghee, olive oil, avocado oil
- Some approved pre-packaged whole food compliant meals, in moderation

Non Whole Foods

- Processed meats with added sugars, sulfites, MSG, or carrageenan
- Surimi (fake crab) sticks, processed fish and fish products with added sugars, sulfites, MSG, or carrageenan
- All dairy products, including milk, cheese, butter etc. Also non-dairy creamers
- Junk food, including 'healthy' junk food
- All sugars and sugar substitutes including honey, stevia, agave syrup, coconut sugar, etc.
- All grains, including gluten free grains
- Legumes, including all beans, peas, chickpeas, lentils, and peanuts
- Spice mixes with sugars or sulfites, MSG, carrageenan
- Sodas and sugar-added juices, alcohol in any form
- Pickled items
- Soy products, including soy milk, soy sauce
- Vegetable oil, peanut oil, mixed oils

Remember the golden rule: If in doubt, leave it out!

Printable Weekly Menu Planner

CPSIA information can be obtained
at www.ICGtesting.com
Printed in the USA
LVHW02s0902100318
569390LV00004B/152/P